Heidi & The Reds

and other adventures of Austin, Texas

By

Mel McCabe

ISBN: 1-4033-2498-0

Library of Congress Control Number: 2002091577

This book is printed on acid free paper.

Printed in the United States of America
Bloomington, IN

Cover art by Tom McCabe

1stBooks - rev. 08/13/02

To Darren Engh,
And Evelyn Haddad -
My comrades in arms,

- and to Ted, and Tom Waits,
for *Raindogs,*
because
we are all raindogs too.

Austin, Texas

She says "seament" and the
sunset becomes Southern.
Now the pole I twist around,
the decision I mull around,
the fear I revolve around,
stems from Texas-
And I go there, crying
about the heat, twelve days of summer
at 100 plus, heavily outweighing the twenty-four
advantages on my list of pro's and con's.
So I scan the list again
finding myself
back in the wicker chair
of the Cuban café-
Outdoor rainbow tiki lights
strung in the stretch of a star
from elm to elm, flicker brighter
than "safety" and the "good transit system,"
number six and fourteen.
Subtle hand held coffee cups
filled with spicy chai and chamomile
healing Peruvian flues, fostering fertility,
add more atmosphere,
push us out the door,
distancing us from family
to come to this lone star state.
I leave my Western fears
to find Southern ones,

yet to find solace in the sequins
of the singer's dress -
turning like 3000 disco balls, little
suns casting specters of light
onto her neck.
And the bassist's suit has tiny
black lines, cobwebs in my home-mind movie-
I am the spider spinning the web
on his pant,
brushed away between sets.
Yet my poetry
does make you nervous,
does crawl into your head
as I break away from
the unknown narrator.
"What are you writing?" -
"Oh Nothing."
"You make me nervous."
"I know."
But when you fear me, you
do not take away pieces of my fear
as I thought you would.
I continue to repeat what you say
(only on paper) until you scream
"STOP!" like a six-year-old child,
sick of the copycat game.
But it is too late -
I've immortalized you.
The way your hair sticks up
on the back of your neck
is now a poem

is now a trend
is ready to be copied.

Networking the Planet

It just wouldn't seem right to begin a book of short stories without first laying out the groundwork of just what in fact led us down to the sleepy Southwestern town of Austin. It also wouldn't be fair to lead readers to believe that such stories that are about to unfold sprang up instantaneously, without a bewildering period of not having a clue as to what the new city of our choice had to offer. I must give sole credit to the annual music festival, *South by Southwest* for truly introducing my cousin and I to all that is Austin. I must also not forget or ignore what our lives were like before that festival, the hibernation period, the workaholic stage and of course the winter of the "five ninety-nine pie special" of Marie Calendar's of which we took full and daily advantage.

1

How we actually blew into town isn't incredibly difficult to explain, although if you took a poll at work, you'd think we were the biggest loons alive. People down here don't tend to leave, the ones who grew up here I mean. I could say that they really have little reason to uproot, with the public parks and clubs, nightlife in general that gives New Orleans a run for her money, radio stations that let you in on all the town's local talent and secrets, and more restaurants and movie theaters per capita than any other metropolitan city in the country. Although it is not fair to wonder why any given individual would want to leave Austin, because the two of us did the unheard-of, in fleeing one the most gorgeous towns on the planet. San Francisco is a brilliant invention of God as well, yet the excuse for leaving that near utopia of liberality has more to do with economics than anything else. Not only do natives of the Bay Area find themselves competing against other transient Californians for good jobs and low-priced housing, but the rest of the planet who is anxious to test the theory on the world-renowned charm and romance the city has to offer as well. I could save you a plane trip, a bus trip, or a long hitchhiked trek to San Francisco if you would only believe me now, it is as fabulously charming as any book, magazine or friend has ever told you. But you will ignore me, undoubtedly, and the already depleting one percent vacancy housing-market, will close to zero before the end of the decade. So I am gone, to a town who will not bleed me for nine-hundred dollars a month for a studio, where I can only pray my face will stop twitching at the twelfth night in a row of Top Ramen a la hot plate.

Is the picture colorful enough for you or shall I continue? In fairness, economics has never been a sole reason for anything in my life, often the completely irrational motives have proved greatest in their forceful ways of pushing me out of the nest or far enough from my harbor of comfort ability. Viv and I spoke with a friend last night who summed up so many reasons for me leaving the beautiful homestead of the coast. He said, "I guess I'll head back up North after graduation. I mean I've already done a lot of networking up there and it's comfortable." Viv looked as though she was gonna wretch upon his statement and I in fact felt sorry for him, because you know, it is truly his prerogative to wanna go back home and re-light the fires that hath burned in high school. Viv and I think alike though, which has undoubtedly kept us friends for as long as people have wondered what paired the two of us together beyond familial affiliation.

We don't wanna be comfortable, or ever become that way in fact. Yes, I know I am striving for a certain kind of safety, for which I do not know if I have ever felt. Although, I would settle upon finding that in a man, a big strong Grant Hill, Detroit Piston's type, but never within the drawn lines of a geographical location. To Viv and I, I suppose that kind of safety represents stagnancy and stagnancy alludes to the cessation of growth and the end of growth means death. Is the melodrama of George shining through before page three? I do feel sorry for you, but you must adapt to be able to go on any further. The second problem with our dear friend's statement (who one may wonder if he so wishes to be our friend as of late printing) was the whole idea of networking. Let's face

3

it. The three of us are twenty-four, Viv, me and our friend that is. And in all reality, our friend possesses the true maturity level of a fifteen-year-old (a fact that I would have no problem disputing in his very presence so do not add 'bitchy attitude' to the list beginning with melodrama as to qualities of the narrator to which are already grinding your nerves). Who the hell wants to talk networking in his or her twenties? We might as well add, retirement plan, medical benefits, college savings for the kids and life insurance while we're at it. I must apologize if you're a networker, a schmoozer and plan-ahead kind of girl or guy, but I know that I never wanna get started, not before I get the chance to just begin my great adventure and that is how this whole thing swings around full circle.

My childhood next-door neighbor got married last weekend. The limo pulled up on Saturday and out of her parents house she walked, veil, white pumps, dress with train and all and my mother stood beside my father on the inside of their kitchen staring out the beveled window in disbelief. Why were they not invited? Shist! My mother was practically her godmother for crying out loud and then my mom told me.

"Well you heard what I said to her six months ago when she told me about her engagement?"

"No, mom, what happened?"

"Well, I'm not sorry I said anything. I just asked her when she was gonna have time to begin her adventure now."

"You mean you said that, just after she announced to you her engagement?"

"Yes, Georgia. That's what I asked. I mean that girl had the world in the palm of her hand and she was so smart and wanted to travel and conquer the world."

"Well, maybe she just wants to get married."

"I dunno. I just *do not* know."

I thought about what my mother had told her. I could never have been so bold or maybe even have thought it my place to say so, although, I am also not thirty years our neighbor's senior with a wealth of life experience within me. I knew on some levels my mom was right, hell I'm her daughter, her creation. I believed wholeheartedly in the necessity of adventure, the quest for knowledge, but I also believed that some people would only go so far as they believed themselves capable. I think that no matter how fucked up of a job you think your parents may have done in raising you (and let's face it, which ones were given the instruction manual or would have had the time to read it?) if they taught you that there are no limitations on your capability then they did *everything* right. Viv and I walked away with that knowledge, amongst all our other quirks and malfunctions that we wish we could send back to the gods for repairs. And believe me, if I'm pegged the melodramatic bitch, Viv will prove to have a few defects before the book's end. Yet, we know we are capable of conquering no less than, the world. We have begun our grand adventure. We are foraging the country for fortune, the treasures of stories for which we will tell our granddaughters and watch their faces light up in awe at the fact that Nanna did THAT! For us, I know that the escapades of the planet will have a hard time ending after marriage, for how does one put an end to a cycle of venturing that hath begun, by that time, a decade before. *How does one call off her own search party for her soul?* It only ceases when she has filled her core to the point of exploding with every jewel of treasure upon the planet and so it ends when the gods call her number. We will be married and be venturing, having children and exploring, having grandchildren and learning, learning that our lives do yearn for a sense of comfort ability. And so I must lastly apologize to our brash friend, so anxious to go home to Northern California. He never fails to end a call with the question, "When are you guys coming back home and gonna grow up and settle down?" For this I must answer, never. I will find my home in my heart, maybe on the road, maybe in New Orleans, Paris, or even Austin. I will network across the Mediterranean, the Aegean, and the Gulf of Mexico. I will never grow up, never settle upon anything or anyone, but I will become comfortable, comfortable in my one constant - change. For us, the adventure will never end, for us we can always rest easy in the comfort of change.

I suppose I have left little room for questioning our motives for moving away from home. There may be greater intrigue in our choice of cities, whereupon I will exhaust that answer as well. Viv wants to go to Medical School. If you think that the only reason people move out to California is due to the weather and liberal political views, you would have to be delusional. They move there for the ocean, with stars in their eyes and the belief that oranges fall from the trees and that Spielberg will be sure to cast them in ET part two once he lays eyes on their mugs. They'll use any excuse they can get and Medical School is actually a viable one. Unfortunately not only does that leave California residents scrambling for housing and employment, but now the positions to our universities. Of course, our sunshine state wouldn't even think of making life easier by giving any sort of preferential treatment to its natives, instead it is one of the few states in the country that welcomes applicants from all over the world. Texas, on the other hand, pays ominous reverence to its residents. Other than California, New York and Illinois, it has the most Medical Schools in its state and if you've spent a winter in the Midwest or on the East Coast than there is no small wonder as to why Vivian chose the lone star state over Chicago or NYC. In just one year, with a voter registration card, a Texas license plate and a valid address it is simple enough to declare oneself a resident and with that, access into one of the seven Medical Schools in the state.

Now the question becomes, 'How did the crazy cousin come to ride the coattails of the over-achieving second party?' Hence the answer, 'Why not?' In reality, I think I may have influenced a decision or two further than a ride upon any coattails, as Viv might have found herself living in that windy Illinois metropolis if I so had not discouraged against the black snow of sometimes Spring. Giving even more truth to how it all started, I had my own serious doubts as to the livability of a town deep in the heart of the Bible Belt. So I came out and visited. What I saw shocked the hell out of me. It wasn't New Orleans, it wasn't Miami, it sure wasn't New York, but then did I really want it to be? I wouldn't get a thing done in a town that had liquor running down its cobblestone streets. I couldn't speak a word of Spanish and who the hell could afford a pad anywhere in Manhattan or wanted to settle for taking the train in from Jersey?

Austin offered me a whole lot more than merely being a town that didn't have the draw backs that others did. Once again, it wasn't just about economics either. It was about brightly painted buildings, street festivals, good coffee, bohemian breakfast spots, cranberry pancakes, cheap fast sushi, independent movie houses, public springs, and accents not quite as deep as those from Dallas, but just drawling enough to draw one in. So there it began, flying back home from Austin to Phoenix to San Francisco. I thought of ways to tell people that their poster child for flower power and all that makes the streets of San Francisco liberal and positively still the city of love and total tolerance, was moving to the state that believes a short prison sentence and a lethal injection stand for the same thing. It started with the need to correct every person who said, "You're not really moving to the South are you?"

"Of course not," I'd answer back, "Texas is clearly part of the South*west*!" but I was only fooling myself. How much further toward the Arctic pole does the United States get than Texas? Florida? After awhile, I stopped taking offense and becoming touchy. Inflicting shock, by announcing my move, became a delightful way to invoke humor in an otherwise tedious day. I mean how many of my Midwestern schoolmates from college had a whole slew of California stereotypes for which I had left unfulfilled? Just as I was not the surfer, fluff-puffed, cheese eating yoganonda, I had to believe everyone in Texas would not be donning a gun rack atop of their horn-rimmed monster truck, a beer, and a confederate club card. I was right, aside from the fact that I have yet to meet a Texan who cannot describe the decor of the inside of a Travis or Williamson County jail cell, no stereotyping has rung true.

Our first apartment was leased with haste as my worry was vast at having to keep our cars which housed our lives, in the parking lot of a one star motel until the apartment finder could find us a find. Although apartment finders back in the Bay Area are rare and never free, our first one in Austin left much to be desired. Her scare tactics brought out the fear in me and the anger in Vivian. If I had to hear one more utterance alluding to the slim likelihood of the two of us being able to find anything with no jobs already lined up, I thought I was going to throttle the woman. Vivian, on the other hand was resting assured on our rental history, the fact that we had both been saving up since our decision to move five months prior and had only to have our accounts checked to find an easy four months resting in advance. June, the finder was not convinced and pushed Vivian with her negative vibes until she was fired, if free service employees can be terminated. In any event, her services were not rendered. We found Shirley the next day and another fifty dollars at the one star later. We signed at the second place we saw, which in retrospect, (three days later) was thought of as a rash decision.

The apartment itself was nice enough, although we were both so unfamiliar with the market that we opted for a cheap one-bedroom thinking we could not afford a two bedroom. I almost failed to mention the one bath part as well. I moved my carload into the breakfast nook and cardboarded up the bar-hole where the stools might have gone to create an additional bedroom with the help of an Asian room divider, compliments of the Salvation Army. I don't think that we ever really realized how small our apartment was (in fact, some six hundred square feet if I can remember correctly), but that may be mostly in part to the fact that our backs were hurting far too much.

There's no way around saying it - I'm cheap. Vivian is cheap too, but together we are the cheapest of the cheap. There is another element to our madness. Yes, in part we did not want to purchase beds because we did not have the money, but in full I did not know how long I was going to last out in Texas and did not want to accumulate so much that it would have been impossible to fit it back into my car and high-tail it back home. The purchase of a sock would have put me in the van rental stage, considering how full to capacity I had packing the car to move. All insanity now divulged, we came up with the brilliant idea of buying seventeen dollar camping air mattresses and sleeping our first six months on them until we were more familiar with our long-term plans. Our long term plans proved to include none other than infinite chronic back pain. Poor Viv's mattress acquired a slow leak the first week and she spent the better part of the evenings of the next five months adding air to whatever might have remained until morning, into the plastic bed. To top off our thriftiness, we steered away from the practical auto-pump for fifteen dollars, which would have done the job in five minutes a night and opted for a two dollar and ninety-five cent basketball pump. This was later thrown against the wall in anger, leaving us with nothing but blow dryers on cold air pressed to the lip of the bedside. We waited until we had both pulled each and every muscle in our backs before insisting upon buying beds, which we ended up finding for less than two hundred each at a furniture outlet. Averaging as we did later, to have been sensible in the beginning, it would have cost us less than a buck a day, minus the pain. Although I stick firmly to the belief that the only thing worse than being comfortable is being sensible, on those air mattresses we were neither.

It was not all the fault of the beds that we did not sleep much those first few months in Austin. Oddly enough though, for how little sleep was achieved, very little sightseeing was done as well. As anyone knows who happens to blow into town without knowing a soul or having a job secured, it becomes very difficult to become acclimated as to the hot locale of entertainment. We opted then to pour ourselves into work. Viv's situation proved somewhat lucrative as she quickly met many other Texans in her position of geographic convenience (the retirement home just down the street). I, on the other hand, began my work on the all-American novel, writing hour after hour, only removing my headphones long enough to shovel a wee bit of Mac and Cheese into my jowls and then begin typing away again. Three months later, at the end of the book, it was agreed that Viv and I had scarcely seen one another. I had indeed grown curious about the place in which she had been hiding herself. There was little to resolve the situation, but find the quickest way for me to replenish the writing fund and gain access once again to my cousin's presence, but begin working at the retirement home as well.

Viv punched in on the clock as a medical supervisor and I found the facility needing another body to fill an apron in the kitchen. So October, November and December were spent with very expeditious amounts of time away from the facility, frequent double-shifts and even a Thanksgiving at the place. We both agreed that having not yet met anyone outside of work and not knowing where to shake our booties, it was best to store up the funds and be where we were terribly needed. Working in the kitchen proved to be the hardest job I ever had or ever would have for that matter, yet I brought some of the difficulty upon myself in my need to prove my strength and break the record as the fastest dishwasher this side of the Mississippi. Viv enjoyed her end of the bargain and became very close to many of the residents, proving her boundless love for the elderly, befriending even the food thrower, resident pervert on wheels and the man who loved to water the plants with his penis. Anytime we were able to escape was spent either sleeping or eating. To make matters easier, we saved our backs by abandoning our beds toward the end of our lease and opting for sleeping bags in the living room. This was closer to the television, the food and the door so that we could fall right into bed after one foot was placed inside the apartment. Our sleep patterns became incredibly bizarre as shifts would sometimes start at four in the morning and others end at six. The problem back at the apartment became fear of injuring oneself in bed as a fork or knife would commonly be left next to a sleeping bag if one was too tired to get up after she ate and fell asleep with utensil in hand or mouth.

That first lease, in that tiny apartment worked for us. Sometimes you don't notice the drawbacks of a place when you are so excited about the venture itself. Part of those six months was spent as a hibernation period, for me writing, for Viv within the walls of work. The theater provided the one place where we could not only escape from the heat, but sit comatose in our tired and tattered states of mind. I don't think I've ever seen so many movies in all my life and can attest to the fact that Viv had never. Now I insist upon her seeing every one of the nominated flicks up for the Oscars, but we tend to spread them out a little. We ate, lord did we do our part in exploring every steak spot in the greater Austin area and became fast friends with red meat, something that is more difficult for a Californian than one might imagine. I can honestly say that there is more Texas in each of us than I ever thought possible. I don't even know if Viv will stay out here for Med School. She may move further East in her explorative, 'never settle back home' sort of way. I, on the other hand, just might find myself making this once thought so foreign, Southern town my home. I think the coffee got to me or maybe it was the heat working against my better judgment, but don't go thinking that I have succumbed to the prophecy of our frequent phone-calling friend. I don't expect to see the day I will retire my traveling shoes and as far as losing my comfort in change, well I just couldn't live with that. I do know though that there is life outside of California. You come out here and you even lose sight of the economical reasons for leaving. If talent and charm could be harnessed, I do believe there are more than a handful of singers in these downtown Sixth Street clubs that like a certain piper, could lead the children out of town and up into the mountains as if by magic.

I have tended to spread my comfort capabilities around as of late, remember there are no limitations on my capabilities and the comfort I am putting in Austin was a feeling I used to think I would only reserve for one other city of vast romanticism. I am beginning to understand that it becomes almost possible to put an end to the ties that bind one to a place if she so allows herself to stay longer than a few weeks. The feeling I used to reserve only for Austin has become an appreciation for this entire state. I don't know as if Viv or I ever thought that we would become Texans, feel our hearts swelling at the passing of a blowing lone star flag or insist upon attending the rodeo and buying a new pair of boots every few years. Who knows? Maybe the only status achievable is 'honorary Texan.' They take this seriously out here to be sure. I don't think that either one of us have it in us to convince the other that lives of potential stagnancy exist for us, particularly in our twenties. Although, I have noticed that we have acquired thrice the amount of furniture and clothes than will ever fit neatly back into our cars without thinking twice about moving further than fifty miles from our Southern Bohemia.

Our trips to the thrift stores are more frequent, my need to create the appearance of a home of comfort ability has become so convincing it almost makes me believe I am staying and yet a single call from our friend and I could be moving. It would be easier than I can even imagine for one to mock me into jetting off, venturing again in the manner I have still reserved for my cross-country travels of summer and European treks through London at Christmas time. Our Sunday night hangout and our favorite sushi bar will not bolt me to the Texas earth or terminate my wandering ways. At this point, Vivian would not allow me to compromise. I remain far from the day I will enter my own limo in my not so white, but equally stunning wedding dress and so the adventures must continue. For what would there be to write?

Someday I am quite sure, if God allows, Viv will be making the rounds in her white lab coat. I will be sitting back watching my epic novel climb to the top of the bestseller's list. We will laugh at the possibly impetuous and naive ideas we may call youth, although that is indeed the point at which I wish to press upon. If the unexpected and innocent motives are reserved for the youth, than think them and live them or all will be wasted and left without adventure, without change. Until then we hang our lab coat and impending fame upon hooks at the back of our closets, rest easy in our capabilities and aggressively network the planet, beginning with Texas.

Mel McCabe

Bugs and the Wind

They were almost the reason I got back into the car and drove straight home, but I didn't. Sucking back my tears and clenched my nails into the palms of my hands, I remembered Kasey and how she had survived those two years down along the Ivory Coast where they are said to be the entire size of an adult man's hand including all four of his fingers and a thumb. They fly too. Not just down in Africa, they fly out here too. I'm not a complete sissy, if they couldn't fly or maybe leap and jump as well, I would not play the part of the damsel in distress, but as they are, remains a reason to get back into the car and move home.

When I spotted the first one, I convinced myself that our complex might be privy to them, not that consolation was found in thinking our brand new home was infested, although venturing out into the rest of the city looked more alluring. All calming interest in the rest of the town dispersed upon discovering they were not confined to the complex alone. Crawling out from under the bushes, pushing their scarabed bodies out from beneath the earth, creeping on and around the scabbed bark of the trees, they were everywhere. Black, brown, shiny gray, eyes that glared and antennas and thick thighs that rubbed so viciously in their hunger for blood, I could hear them calling to me, humming that incessant scream of the bug banshee, warning me, mocking me, causing every hair that fluttered onto my forehead in the night to become subject to a smack of my hand every five minutes for fear that it had to be a roach versus a lock.

There were so many reasons for not making the trek out to Texas that I can hardly count, but I had carefully listed out the pro's and con's and was left with convictions that pointed to only one choice - the lone star one. In all my background checks that included the evaluation of the transit system, malls, and Chinese restaurants, I had missed one thing, the ratio of creepy-crawlers to that of humans and baby, we were outnumbered.

There was no escape, no amount of *Off* or insecticide that could eliminate the truth. It wasn't just the heart of the state or that town and the two to the East. It was the heat. It was the June, July, August, and let's face it, September, that clung to you like undried staticy hotpants fresh out of the wash. It was summer in Texas and it was the season of the bugs. The first solution seemed simple. I never liked shorts anyway and by constantly clothing myself in long jeans, I minimized the odds of large bugs leaping onto my skin. But if you haven't lived in Texas then you are the only readers not laughing because long jeans in July become as probable a tactic as one fearing the loss of her tan in the Arctic and therefore donning a string bikini every day of winter. It was too damn hot for pants. Ravaging the Salvation Army for short skirts because I really do not do shorts, I completed my new Texas appearance with open toe sandals and therefore opened the curtain on the first scene of 'The Insecting.' And they came, they flew to my skin, into my toeless shoes and onto my ankles and I had no choice but to go ballistic.

Thoughts of moving home subsided though, thoughts of leaving the apartment did as well. As we tried to jam the new couch (also from the local Salvation Army) into the narrow doorway of old apartment number one fifteen, Muhammad sauntered out of number one seventeen and said, "Hey ladies."

"Hi, howya doin'?"

"You guys need any help?"

Yeah, about thirty-six boxes, two desks, and two dressers ago, Muhammad, I thought in my mind. "Na, we're doing okay. Listen, Muhammad, are there always so many bugs here?"

"Oh, yeah. I guess so. This is not more than usual."

"Do they ever get into your apartment?"

"No. No. You've always got to make sure you keep your AC lower than 70 and they won't come in. They like the heat."

And so began an era of chilling temperatures and sanity regained, at least within the sanctity of our home. Turning the air conditioning on, for the Queen of the Cheap, is an act almost as heart-wrenching as accepting that you are a minority subspecies among the majority bug population. I did it though, not due in part to the loosening of my ultra-tight money clip, but largely because of Viv's father. You see, I only need to hear so many horror stories regarding bugs before I am harbored incapacitated with the mind saturation of four-legged nightmares.

It makes no difference to me that the scene was set in Jordan, I seriously doubt that roaches have such varying personalities that the Middle Eastern variety prove so different from their Texas cousins. Viv's father also found himself in the swallow of a throat of heat so great that it felt as though it would never be washed down and yet evidently the comforts of an air-conditioned apartment were not obtainable. He too was awakened in the middle of the night, but with little to counter his bug beliefs, as his hair was not long enough to touch down upon his forehead. It was not a bug though that rose him from his slumber. It was a black sheet of some five thousand bugs, roaches and hoppers, mantises, and spiders alike that had congregated to his torso, to his face, nearly down into the crevices of his mouth, had he been one to snore. He survived. Actually, he might not be pleased at my truth telling, yet he professed to run screaming out of his house to the next-door neighbors, two women who led the way back with brooms in hand. These women scurried and brushed the insects out from his bed single-handedly, in a way I never could. Although these women give pride to my gender, I stick hard to my belief that men will never prove obsolete for two reasons, one being the fact that we will always need bug killers, the other being quite obvious. The garbage will always need taking out.

Like Vivian's father though, that summer, I too became a survivor. And it is not enough to say that we come out alive and kicking through the events we are forced to live through. My life is no longer about self-sacrifice or survival, it's rather about knowing that I have a choice in all matters and whether I want to live with the bugs or not. I decided that I did. You see, the list of pro's and con's somewhere along the line gets cast to the wind. Whether you are looking at a paper that has thirty pro's to one con or an even twelve and twelve, if that one con is so horrible that you cannot sleep at night than it has a way of outweighing the plethora of pro's. In Texas my one con, didn't lie heavier on the grand scale, although I remember a time and place when one con did.

It was the winter of ninety-two, Chicago, the great blizzard and all it took was the wind to blow me away. Throughout the late seventies, the eighties, that one year in the nineties, I had been a Californian sleeping my life away on the dreams of becoming a Midwesterner. I was ready to enter into a population of sturdy stock, all-American cars, a meat and potatoes girl with wholesome values, and the belief that Hollywood and LA were the denizens of crazy people. I prepared myself to become lost in the cornfields of Illinois, to farm Indiana and build my own home upon one of the lakes of Michigan where I would die a happy woman. And so I found myself, trekking two thousand miles, two time zones, and half a country away from the Pacific Coast to begin my adjustment, to begin fooling others that I, the native Californian, born of two Midwesterners had lived in Chicago all my life. But three summers, one mild winter visit out to Grandma and Gramps, and a rather thin goose-down Eddie Bauer fashion jacket did not prepare me for that winter. Nothing could have prepared me for that fall and of course the spring that really never came. It all might have worked out differently if the snow had not begun to fall in October and maybe if it might have chosen to let up earlier than the twenty-sixth of May, but I doubt it.

You see, all geographical locations have a pitfall, all towns including the tiny ones that don't even make it onto the map, have a fault. It is your job to evaluate whether or not you can live with the potential earthquake, hurricane, tornado, tidal wave, volcano, heavy rain percentage, heat wave, cold front, smog fumes, bug population, fog, rodent infestation, simple gossiping Betty or the pure factor that you may be too far away from your family. I used to think that I did not choose to stay in Chicago because I was too far away from home, but that wasn't it. It was the wind. In a normal winter season, things might have turned out differently, but into that winter of ninety-two crept the loneliness bugs, the ones that fester outside of those parka, scarf, ear-muffed people who cannot be determined as females or males. At the end of eight months of nodding at passing snow people, you have discovered that it was in fact too cold to even meet another human, stick your gloved hand out of your still cold pocket to shake a hand or smoke a cigarette. That cab that nearly hit you crossing the icy corner of Wabash yesterday morning was the last straw. You grip and shake your already frozen pepper spray in the bag on your lap that sits on the subway and wonder how many times you can get bronchitis in one season and how the hell you thought you'd fool people into believing you were a Chicago native. Because to them, that cold is probably a little uncomfortable, but to a native Californian it is simply unnecessary and the choice becomes easy, you leave.

Back in California, you smile at the Midwesterners who considered moving home after the LA quake and rest easy in the con's of non-natives until you once again grow restless. Days later and a fourteen hundred mile U-Haul ride away, you find yourself standing in line at the Cineplex deep in the heart of Texas, surrounded by dozens upon dozens of leaping roaches mustering up all the courage you have not to embarrass Vivian among the not so petrified Texans with a tumultuous howl. Before you know it, the theater proves to be the true safe asylum of a Texas summer. They have the AC blustering at such force that your eyelashes form icicles and sweatpants and a sweatshirt prove the necessary uniform. Viv and I found that we would, on an average Saturday, enter the place at noon and vacate the building at no earlier than eleven that evening in sheer attempts to avoid the swelter of a one hundred and three degree day, and of course its inhabitants.

Is it any small wonder that the fourth definition of a bug in the Webster's Dictionary is 'a defect or a problem?' Although that definition does not intend to pertain to one of insectual nature, bugs are a problem, a defect of the planet and yet not as harrowing as the wind. Because the wind taught me very little. The wind blew me away and played close to the team of Chicago citizens who might not have wanted any more crazies from the sunshine state to filter into their voting booths and take away their jobs by birthright. All the wind taught me was that the dreams of a young girl might exist very separately from the reality from which they stem. I no longer build massive and extravagant fantasies based upon what I only imagine a place or its people to be like. I am not any weaker of a woman for not withstanding the wind nor am I any less of a survivor for not staying any longer than a year. Because a year can be a long time, indeed an excruciating long period in an eight-month hibernation of a crowded dorm room. Then there comes a time, usually after about a year, when you must ask yourself if it is as important to be 'sticking it out' and 'surviving' as it is to pick a climate, terrain or other town in which one might no longer find herself crossing off the winter days on her calendar and find herself thriving. I must amend the aforementioned statement that 'the wind taught me nothing,' for it indeed did me some good. The wind blew me down to Texas.

It proves ironic, but the first words expelled to us out of our cars from our first (and not last) apartment finder were, "So you girls think you can just *blow into town* with no plans?"

And I remember thinking to myself, 'That is exactly what we think.' We *blew into town*. Viv rode the softer breeze of the warm Santa Ana from LA and I jumped aboard the blizzard of Chicago back home to California, twisting down South, to where we both met up, Texas. It was indeed those winds of change that brought us here and it was the bugs that had me pondering just how long I wanted to stay.

"Viv? Do I wanna raise my kids out here with all these bugs?"

"Well, you don't have to be thinking kids as of yet. Do you? I mean give it three months, they're not gonna be here in the winter."

"The kids?"

"Nah, the bugs!"

And they weren't. The winters down here make you forget there are such things as creepy crawly beady-eyed black beetles. The winters make you wonder how you ever thought yourself a future Midwesterner as you lounge out by the pool in the eighty-degree warmth of the sun. And then it begins to get hotter, the humidity soars, the daily temperatures rise and your ears become sensitive to the faint sound of an incessant humming, growing louder, from the tops of the trees, from under the earth, from right underneath your goddamn lounge chair! It's spring.

As I watch the bug, paralyzed with fear, wondering how apt it is to get stuck onto my ankle or thigh, currently drenched in the oil of half a bottle of Hawaiian Tropic, I realize that I am so afraid of the little bugger because I am incapable of killing the damn thing. The phobia stems back to that summer night back at age sixteen up on that dark highway headed toward Tahoe when all that lay between me and the casinos were one hundred and eight miles and a raccoon in the center of the divide. As I swayed as far left as possible, he too, darted for the left and I flew directly over the hairy beast. I can still see the eyes of the creature just before impact and recall how the car jumped a good two feet into the air after having flown over the body. Pulling over, some twenty feet up on the side of the highway, I warned my paranoid delusions against another thought of the ghost of the beast floating up off the road to come and get me. Puking in the manzanita bushes, beside my car, I wiped my mouth on the wrapper of an old sucked blow pop, before getting back into the car and crying the rest of the way on up to Caesar's. The revelation of never being able to kill anything larger than a flea after that night was the only good that might have come out of that experience. For I can still sense the blame that all the raccoon ancestors of the deceased place on me when looking into my eyes as I still encounter one on a rare trip out to the trash can. This may explain my imperative requirements regarding trash duty and insect watch patrol for the future hubby.

I am left to stare at the roach, now perched at the edge of my lounge chair, looking up at me in a half-cocked, ready to pounce kind of smirk. I believe that I am not as frightened as I was during the encounters with the mangy creatures of the Southwest. There was nothing left but room for improvement between my insectual relations and me when considering my initial psycho squeals of terror. I think I may have even learned something from the bug. Every late spring that branches out into the blistering heat of the summer carries with it a million little creatures, beings that force me to come to terms with my fears or risk shaving off another year of life in the stress-laden existence of this twenty-four-year-old. And I will not have it. The loss of another year that is.

I fight the fear. Because it all starts with the bugs. For every person who journeys to a town in which he or she has not been born, there is something for which to adjust. If you can, come to terms with the possibility of that tornado, the probability of that earthquake, the frequent meetings with those bugs, then you have gained something - a little more courage. For in reality, the only being unafraid of anything is the being or beings who created this planet. For every dream that lies dormant in the hearts of all beings in this universe, there is a reason for which that vision remains fettered. It is fear. For every stage I wish to stand upon, for all the songs I need to be sung, for each poem I yearn to read out loud, for every man to whom I wished I could have told those three words, there stands only one thing in the way - fear. But the bugs bring me closer, closer to shedding the inherent trepidation of my species, closer to waving goodbye to the wall of apprehension that stands in the way of each and every fantasy to which I intend upon giving substance. Those shiny black scarabs of this lone star state hop upon my shoe, no longer mocking me, but reminding me that even as a child there came a time to banish the nightlight to the attic and embrace the darkness. The roaches fly to the right of me, to the level of me, at eye left, forcing me to swallow my scream and reminding me that they will always be here, but I will too. In conquering my fear of the bugs, in choosing Texas over its minute seasonal inhabitants, I prove to love those repulsive creatures more fervently than I did the wind. I come closer to standing center stage, singing, bellowing my poems to be heard upon the highest rooftop, echoing the words, "I love you," and all because of the bug.

Some evenings now, when I'm seated outside on the deck of a downtown café, wondering if the air is in fact hotter than the brown sugar liquid at the bottom of my coffee cup, for a fleeting moment I find myself closing my eyes and sloping into that icy Chicago wind. But then the moment does just that, fleets and blows away. A cockroach vaults up onto my table. He winks at me, mocks me, and smiles because he knows that I am incapable of killing him. He is the bane in my side and at the same time the reason I stay. He is the reason for remaining in my chair, in this heat, in this city that carries with it such charm. He is the very link in the chain that binds me to the lone star state, fettered and yet becoming a little less afraid.

Porthole to a Cuban Cafe

She had these black stars permanently burnt into her sternum. It's hard to be certain, relying solely on my memory, but I see five of them, at about a sand-dollar-size apiece, which is massive when you consider the length at which a branding tool or needle must singe or poke at the thin flesh that covers your bones just above your chest. I imagine that most customers on any given day get a pretty good look at those stars remembering how sweltering hot it always seems to be inside the place any night in spring, summer or fall. Hell, this last winter was even tank top material. Most nights they wheel out that fan. It's the largest fan I've ever seen, but a fan in the middle of a room really only manages to regenerate the already heavy sticky air right back at ya. No, I remember it never fails to move your hair around a whole bunch as well. Pushing your

29

bangs up from their 'smashed to their forehead' status, to a straight up in the air salute to all new friends you had planned on meeting for the night and now never will.

It is not as important for me to meet people when I go out for coffee as it is to surround myself with others, others that for probably very similar reasons can no longer tolerate or be allowed the pleasure of planting their asses on bar stools add infinitum. As far as coffeehouses go, this one gets my vote. I don't really know what makes one coffee joint all that different from another, other than one individual's exceptional taste in wall paint and of course memories. Memories of *that* place may never fail to be sparked by first sight of tattooed stars, which are always followed by a trail of Cuban flared walls in indigo, violet, red and sometimes green.

I think of the first night we found ourselves sitting there. Viv's old friend from college had been driving us all around town in hopes of recruiting us in the great move down south from California. That girl had to have been one of the worst drivers with which I had ever driven. I could make myself sick if concentrating too carefully back upon those bumps for which she simply refused to brake and then the stops at which she insisted upon braking, no less than three times each. Five women in a small Volkswagen do not take 'flown over bumps' without a single bump on the head and of course the tall people never fail to end up in the backseat.

It was Spring Break if I remember correctly and every sight before that had been nice, average, quite Berkeliesk and yet for all the comforting comparisons between Austin's bohemian Guadalupe and Berkeley's Telegraph, I had not yet been convinced to begin packing. We had split up the day before. Toni and I took the bus line down Congress and that one antique store nearly pushed me over the edge. A good bargain and a shoebox size store with more merchandise than what should normally fit into a five- family garage had helped to shove me onto the other side of the state border. Now getting across Arizona and New Mexico called for something with a little more finesse. Wholehearted attempts to ignore the beads of sweat that had not ceased to drip down my back in the four days since we had arrived might have even been harder to overshadow.

There seems to be an excessive need for people to see their name's live on, evidenced by the plethora of initial engravings in each and every square inch of public commercialized wood on the planet. I ran my index finger over an 'R' in the name Roberto as I waited for my chai and wondered when people carve their names with the employees standing there all night, or if this was merely an accurate inventory of the employees themselves dating back from either opening or when the last counter top had been replaced. Even though it had to have been close to a hundred degrees, I asked for a hot chai. The girl with the stars gave me a strange look, not a rude strange look, but nevertheless one of curiosity, which surprised me. I thought that people working in a warm climate would have known that the only way to truly cool off in the heat was to drink something hot. I'm serious, you drink something cold and your surroundings become that much hotter. The young man next to her with long blond hair watched her steam the top of the glass as he poured some sort of iced coffee shake and said, "I think she wants a cold chai. The ice is at the bottom of the freezer."

I cast my eyes away from the jars of loose tea, chamomile and Earl Grey and answered back, "No, I wanted a hot chai, really."

"Oh," said the kid and smiled down apologetically as he overfilled his shake by at least fifty percent, only realizing when the foam hit his knuckles.

My hot chai was placed onto the counter. I paid my two fifty and threw the remaining two quarters into the tip jar. At that point in my life quarters were not being solely conserved for laundry. Viv, my sister and the Evil Canevil of four-wheeled vehicle already sat in the corner of the room, under a dimly lit table lamp. Those in search of eminence had not forgotten the tabletop either and this time I looked down at a couple's profession of love, two initials joined by a heart and oddly thought it endearing. There must have been something in the drink stronger than tealeaves to temporarily put an end to my cynicism. I wrapped my hands around the glass, despite the sweat that began to draw faster from my brow and turned my chair toward the stage where three Latin women in their early twenties sat singing and strumming guitars.

They were in no way subject to the comparison of typical coffeehouse entertainers of the Northern California area. I apologize to anyone who might have grabbed a hold of fame from the back room of *Rosa's Coffee Den* in San Jose or even the corner Starbucks in Burlingame, but this charming Texas capital puts an entirely different spin on typical coffee bean entertainment. They were *good*, typically good as I would later find out, because yes, somewhere between the Spanish version of Dylan's 'Gotta Travel On' and that bite of Toni 's homemade apple pie, I decided to travel on myself, move on down to the somnolent charming capital that would soon become my home.

Sipping my chai, I allowed the spices to swim to the back of my throat, not forgetting to first hit the left side of my mouth and delve deep into the pit of my canker soar. It never fails that my mind only chooses to remember that it is that time of the month where period cramps hit you like a sharp knife in the jugular as I take that initial sip of my tea. Chai has got to take the place of number one on the long list of caffeine-laden drinks that only manage to increase cramp pain from minor discomfort to the labor pain status. A man can only understand that kind of anguish if he has had his testicles ripped out one by one and somehow sewn back into place to only await with horrified anticipation the process of them being removed again just twenty-six short days later. Nevertheless, women get used to pain, whether it be by emotional heart standards or that of the physical nature and my eye always manages to spot the bottom of the cup before the pain fully ignites. It is also no secret that I am wildly cheap and two dollars and fifty cents will never find itself lost on the eternal dilemma of which is the worst of the three drugs associated with a women's cycle. The others being chocolate and of course nicotine, evidencing three reasons other than war and the creation of breasts, for God being of the male entity.

Even my cramps that night did not affect me in any negating way. Even when Toni spilled her drink onto Viv's lap, the evening was not spoiled. Although, I think that Viv wouldn't have complained if someone would have dumped a scalding mocha atop her head for all the convincing she was trying to do in persuading me to move. And I can't tell you when it happened, when I first thought out load or out loud in my mind, 'I am moving.' I can't say if it was at the moment that I noticed all the tables in the place painted a different shade of the primary colors in the sixty-four color crayon box or if it weighed heavy on my decision making process that the little Cuban coffeehouse in the capital seemed to be doing a better trade than most bars back home on Saturday nights.

It might have been the music, that song. Dylan lyrics always have their own path to my heart. It could have been the fact that to have looked around at the diverse audience might have convinced one that she had entered a secret porthole into the transverse land of Eclectica, and that's Eclectica, Texas to top it off.

No. I cannot quite put the mark on the time, but the place remains clear in my almost always-blurred retention of events. It was a building with crooked walkup cement steps, slackers sat at the sides of them and leaned outward to let us pass up. Upward led to the music, the hum of voices, friends connecting and re-connecting. I attempted to suck it all in through my unbalanced senses, still balancing after the shock of the last speed bump we had ignored and the bump swelling on top of my head I could not ignore while working to scrape the gum off my shoe (undoubtedly collected originally from the mouth of one of the youthful leaning slackers back at the step).

I thought of how my wooden stilettos had no markings of the youths calling for fame as I stared down at the counter waiting for my chai. I thought of how little attention those branded stars would receive if that woman had so chosen to live in let's say, Juno, Alaska. There were many reasons to fall in love with Texas, all of which I had not thought of before that night, all of which I would have never thought existed before I saw them for myself.

"What the hell are you moving out there for?" inquired my old manager at the bookstore I used to work at back home on Main Street. My eyes spilled over the shelves until they caught on the sign that read 'Romance,' and I remembered that man who had come in the day before with one of those handmade grocery store punch tags. His read, "Published Romance Author," and stuck to a pin attached to the breast of his red Mr. Roger's sweater vest.

"Sir," I said as I rang up his thirteenth Signet romance novel, "What book have you written?"

"Miranda Dreams of Lovers," he answered back with the largest smile I had seen since my twelve-year-old viewing of the Cheshire cat in *Alice in Wonderland.*

"That's great," I told him, "When were you published?"

"Just a few months ago. It took me twenty-three years to write the masterpiece, but let me tell you, it was worth every night I stayed up after work. What a feeling."

I looked back at my manager who undoubtedly expected me to say something like, "Well, Rachel, didn't you know that in Texas you can sling a beer while you drink with your rifle hanging out the other side of your car?" Instead I said, "Change. It's just time for a change…and Texas isn't all that you think it is. It's really something more."

The funny thing was that I wasn't so sure how much I wanted her to know about my new secret state. I didn't know how to explain the singers and the dancers, the colors and the coffee, the stars and the spicy chai, the heat that makes you feel a little warrioresk just for surviving it one more night, and of course that antique shop, that bargain basement mumbo jumbo explosion of a store where Toni had purchased that beautiful butterfly pin. I didn't wanna go and clutter the state all up with a bunch of fast-paced sunny city slickers. Who knew if they would have felt the same? Who knew if they could really appreciate it?

I could. I can tell you right now that not a piece of this land has yet to be taken for granted, not by me. I suppose looking back, that Cuban coffeehouse was indeed the place that made me decide, forced me to change, drank me into decision and pushed me forth in song. But then there's always that nametag, you know the kind, made from the label makers. I mean I stood there after having just come back from Spring Break, remembering the heat and that smell of beer. I will tell you that there is an eternal stench of warm beer that clings to the downtown sidewalks on any giving night of that city, but I stood there. I found myself staring at that "*Published Romance Author*" label stuck to that pin and realized that the ceaseless search for fame was too great for me in California. There, it isn't so much about stabbing your initials into a hunk of wood or sweetly carving a heart into the center of a purple tabletop. It's about letting every single solitary person who walks on past you know that you are an Author, you have made it, you are famous, you have an agent, a publisher, a company, and your very own piece of the corporate world.

I'm not gonna lie, for once. I am, let's not forget, no longer living in the sunshine state and the reasons for lying and conniving out here are few and far between any benefits you might receive from doing so. We don't have the kind of lawyer population they do back home and we don't kill our best friends for parts in movies and screenplay rights. We sit in Cuban cafes and watch the stars. Absent of cell phones, we listen to the Spanish melody of Dylan against the faint drumming of the world's largest fan. Slacker kids smoke outside. You might spend a solid hour doing nothing more than picking the crust from a homemade apple pie out from between your molars and scraping the gum off your shoe as you play gin, connect with friends, stare at the local paintings along the walls and remain mystified at the safety of a coed bathroom with nothing but a shower partition between the stalls.

It wasn't exactly the time or that place, it was more like the exact feeling I obtained at that time and place that had me turning toward Viv and saying, "I'm moving. I mean it this time. I'm ready to move."

She smiled because she didn't have any reason to believe me. How many times had I professed my promise to relocate to Los Angeles? But it was in fact different this time. No one had a way of knowing but me. Los Angeles had the beaches, the Boulevard, the fame so close you gotta watch for it even when you roll your shopping cart down the aisle of Vons. It can come up close enough to bite you in the ass. But shopping at the same grocery store as the Bridges brothers is liable to give someone like me a heart attack. It's prone to go hand in hand with pretension and the awfully annoying reality that it is necessary to apply makeup to merely run out for toilet paper. Let's not forget that a binge on a half-gallon of ice cream is out of the question when you might find yourself next to Tarantino in the ten items or less. See I've already lapsed into the life of the high-stringer just thinking about it.

This time was for real. I thought I might have even known it when I ran my palm over the jellybean Tiffany lamp for thirty-two seventy-five in that old antique store on Congress, but I wasn't, sure that is. As my ass clung to the wood of the chair in the ninety-five degree Texas heat of the Cuban café, I was sure. Because there really aren't enough coffeehouses on the West Coast (I write with a cynical smile), not with the same contradiction of being slowly comforting and with the ability to supply one with the last great drug of hypertension. There are bars, hell San Francisco oozes bars out of every last pore of the city, but show me a place that checks the liquor and the cell phones at the door and gives you a free band to boot. Despite the lack of Northern California's weather perfection, there is a place that welcomes you with faces that lack pretension, conjuring up smiles, allowing you to dissolve into the warmth of its Southwestern charm.

Long after we had moved and Toni had come out to visit, a two-week stay that ebbed into two months, we found ourselves sitting there. Leaning my head against the indigo wall, I told her, "I thought we'd come here cause this place always proves the best backdrop for momentous occasions."

She said to me, so naïve, as little sisters often are, "But what momentous event are we celebrating?"

Sometimes things are better left unsaid, so we just cried because after all it was now about *her* great move, her decision to trek eastward, to New York, her time to say goodbye. I remember she wore that butterfly pin, the one from the old antique store. The rainbow colors of its wings all smeared together as I cried. I thought hard on that pin to try and stop my tears and to free myself from looking at the on-looking, who undoubtedly were wondering which one of us had been diagnosed with a terminal illness. That butterfly pin that I wished I had picked up myself for a dollar when it looked like it was an easy fifty prevented me from screaming out loud, causing sounds of fear and anticipation.

That cafe proved to be the great bay of stay on which to sail to decision and then onto destination. A place that reminds me of a time I did not know what to do and the memory of how I got to where I needed to be. I remember what made me decide to come and fly along those dollar-green golden wings and glide along the Cuban crayon colors of my comfy café.

When Toni got to New York she bought one of those label makers. She made herself a sticker that says, "*I ain't yo bitch*," and wears it on her neon orange Wegman's jacket so that everyone will get a laugh when they see her. It's not the same as forcing your fame on others like the published romance novelist; it's all about humor. A few months ago she sent me one. It says, *"For wings that can fly, I am the greatest published novelist by and by."* To wear it on the outside of my jacket I would have to stick it clear across my back it remains so long. I stuck it instead on the inside, just so that I know, I know my impending fame, to remind myself of my own capabilities, Texas style. Viv and even Toni have yet to discover how much truth is scratching its way through my fiction, how soon I will have to cut the 'novelist' away from my label and become the truth teller.

While we're telling the truth, I suppose I should fess up. I took the butterfly. Visiting my sister back up at college, upstate New York a few weeks ago, jogged all memories of that distant spring break. I discovered an old red sweater, a secretly pilfered one from my own college days in fact, slung over a tall mock doc boot in the corner of her closet. As I was trying it on and then refolding it in classic big sister fashion, my finger touched the edge of a golden antenna attached to the body of a butterfly. The butterfly that I had forgotten until then, being purchased at that same antique store back on Congress that sweltering spring break day in Austin.

I needed the butterfly. I wanted to be reminded of times of indecision, great feats of self-discovery, and the newness and innocence that can become lost in seconds of fleeting moments. Even when I am away, a state that grows more frequent as days grow stale, I need only to close my eyes, lay along the back of my rainbow-clad winged creature and become transformed into my memories of magic tea and apple pie, cards and crying, strumming guitars and Latin female voices, and people coming and going through my porthole to the town of Texas charm. Whenever the skeptic bugs begin to bite, I remember hot spices on my tongue, slackers on the stoop, burnt black stars and butterflies, wooden chairs and table tops, initials of love and those signifying fame, smiles and spills, Viv winning her arguments for moving and finally coming home, but to a home I've never known before, to a refuge of vast solace.

Mel McCabe

Toni Comes Home

I can't pretend to know what it might have been like for you growing up in your family or to judge the degree of perfection regarding the relationships you had with your siblings. If you were an only child, don't even get me started. Some of my best friends in the world have been only children, but the lack of comprehension with respect to the sibling bond is far too difficult to overcome or be even remotely understood for these friends. In my house, growing up, there was the kind of chaos I took for granted as being classically American. The one constant trail of words erupting from the lips of my mother, even above, "Do not air your dirty laundry," was in fact "When your father and I have departed from this planet *that* little girl is the only family you're gonna have, young lady."

Before the age of slight wisdom, that I judge to be twelve, for me, I would scoff at my parents and curse the god who had so mocked me with the gag gift of such a wretched sister. I'm quite sure, in the typical nuclear family way, I detested Toni. Despite the incessant assurance every family friend was bent upon relaying, "You two will be like two pees in a pod in no time, just wait and see," I was less than comforted or convinced.

One must not believe that my detestation ran for reasons less than the pure exercise and angst of it. The kid was no less than a sheer terror. In fact, I do believe that the only time I even felt an emotion close to love for the tike before she turned thirteen, might have been one of sprinkled compassion, that afternoon she met more than her match at nursery school and that shit for brains boy, Joey (the reason for the invention of Ritalin) slammed her underdeveloped hand in a suitcase.

The mania passed down from both of my over-zealous parents was not limited to the torture of me. No, she saw little reason to keep it in the family and devoted much of her time to pissing off each and every friend I brought home as well. The specific incident that never ceases to escape my mind, even after half a decade of best friendom, would have to be the day I brought Kasey home. Kasey to this day remains one of my oldest and dearest friends and after the first day I brought her back to the O'Dell domain, it was a wonder she did not flee the family forever. Toni walked in the room, cute as can aesthetically be, bows in hair, quite the paralleled vision of Rhoda from *The Bad Seed*, to sit herself down in between Kasey and I, who silently scooped up our cereal from our bowls and remained entranced in a brilliant new sub-plot of MacDonald Carring.

"She is so cute," shot out of the mouth of the unknowing Kasey.

Toni smiled and took the admission of her beauty as an ideal time to snag the channel changer. "I wanna watch Smurfs," she yelled as she changed *Days of Our Lives* to an episode of the little blue men.

I rolled my eyes and sat back to watch what my new friend was made of. "That's not gonna work kid," Kasey exclaimed, as she put her cereal on the coffee table and knelt down on the floor, underestimating my sister's prowess.

Just as the channel was successfully switched back to Patch and Kayla's plight of love, Kasey let out a squeal and I cast my eyes off the screen in time to see her cereal bowl hitt her head and the milk spill down, half onto Kasey's locks and half onto the couch.

"Oh, you're gonna get it," I yelled, "You are sooo gonna get it!" I smiled for a second, knowing that it was still my duty to run for a rag and begin to try and get the most smelly spoiled substance of all refrigerated products off the furniture before the shit hit the fan. When I came back with the towel, Kasey had rung the milk from her hair and was once again ensconced in the soap. Toni was nowhere to be seen. After saturating the couch with some detergent and hot water, I too, sat back down, hoping we had heard the last of the runt for the afternoon and she would resolve to play in her room for fear of getting in trouble with Mom. As the hourglass showed 'the second half of *Days of Our Lives* returning in a moment,' Kasey got up to pee. Minutes later, my ears perked up at the sound of clinking, clanking, swearing and screaming coming from the hallway. I jumped up from my spot of the couch to identify what horrors were now taking place. I was met with a scene from midget musketeers as Toni had ambushed Kasey on her way back from the bathroom and was clonking her over the head with one of her batons. Kasey must have spotted another baton from the corner of the room and the two were having at it. Kasey's lack of baton twirling experience put her in the role of the defender, although she was indeed doing most of the swearing. I knew it was only a matter of seconds. As I pleaded with the two of them to cut it out, my mother came running in from the backyard.

"Just what the hell is going on here?" she yelled as Toni dropped her baton and looked up with her puppy dog eyes and juvenile smile.

"This little brat was hitting me with…" Kasey started as my mother stopped her with single hand signal.

Eyes were directed toward my direction and my mother said," Georgia, I don't know what's going on here, but this is not acceptable. I think you know what's happening here and I don't appreciate it one bit." Toni smiled, pranced back into the TV room to watch *The Smurfs*. Kasey and I were banished to my room to sulk and swear our eternal hatred through curses upon who we thought to be devil incarnate.

Hatred did not reign eternal though and much to the surprise of an eleven-year-old, the curse did not stick. The anger melted and the bonding began the day I moved away. She turned thirteen and as all projected, the ardor began to fester in the form of daily letters and bi-daily phone calls from Chicago to San Francisco, San Francisco to Chicago. Through audiotapes of our voices, I taught Toni about music and books, how to perm your hair, cut your hair, color your hair, keep friends, lose friends, write a paper, pick out clothes that others will be sure to detest, shop for a bargain, sing show tunes and memorize every word to *Grease*. She taught me how to take a step away from the fear that had been born to my personality and somehow escaped her's since I slipped from the womb.

There is this picture of Toni. She couldn't be any older than six. She's standing in the snow, wearing a pair of those ridiculous moon boots, my old ones, so they hit her at about knee-level. She is donning a ski coat, one of those sock hats, a pair of mittens and her arms are outstretched like an airplane. Her head is bent upward to the sky with an enormous Cheshire cat grin upon it. It's funny, but whenever I picture Toni, when I'm talking to her on the phone or talking about her to someone else, that's the vision that somehow seems to pop in my head. In that picture, with those hulking moon boots, Toni looks so free, so fearless, ready to fly, jump out over the mountain, above the snow, completely prepared to leave us all and journey onto meeting many others, suck every breath of life up through her nostrils, through each and every pore in her skin. That little six-year-old kid in snow garb never grew up. She became more intelligent, of course. In fact she somehow was able to blow out all the candles on the birthday cakes each year, but without losing any sense of childlike idealism in this often thought corrupt and cynical world in a way most 'intelligent' people will never be able to do. And yet, for her bulldog need to defy danger, for all her twenty-first century heroism that you have to see to believe exists in one so young, for all her boldness, nerve, grit and angelic resolution that I cherish and revere most about her, these qualities solidify why I will never be able to have her near me for very long again. It drives a sister to thoughts of atheism when she sees the irony in how little there was to appreciate for almost a dozen years and then how much there is to hold onto when it can do nothing but slip away. Toni is a free bird, a being dependent upon change and all that the concept invites. She needs to shuffle the cards, turn the leaf, shift the scene, revolutionize, metamorphosize, transform, transpose, tromp the Champs d' Elise as an avatar of France, sail beneath the Ponte Vecchio, dance along the cobblestone of New Orleans, try on every shoe in Soho, meet every person who smiles in the Keys, eat every last lick of ice cream at the truck in Trafalgar Square, innovate another dialect of Spanish along the coasts of Venezuela, take a bath in the public pools of Athens and learn the art of slinging hash in Austin, Texas. Toni never stays. She always goes. She's always caught running, her shoes flipping this way, that way, tripping along every street, always in sets of six-inch platform heels. I taught her something, partly I kept her clean of the chaos, free to become the planet's avatar, the modern day Peter Pan, but mostly she teaches me. I watch her, little me, morphed into a fearless Amazon and I come closer to becoming her everyday. Twins, they used to call us, before I hacked my hair. Even our closest friends at the mall, would stop her or me and call out the wrong name only five feet away. We could fool them. We could not fool ourselves. She walks into danger sometimes and I flee to the safe hollow of old experiences, but together we are, as one man said not long ago, "Those unstoppable O'Dell sisters, taking the world by storm."

For fear of running the risk of teetering into the speech I have yet to write for Toni 's induction into 'The Superwoman's Hall of Fame' in the sky, I will attempt to limit the obvious canonization of 'my sister the Goddess,' from now on to the trials and tribulations of her life with us in Austin. And so she walked off the plane and was greeted with nothing less than happy receptors from a movie. Melodrama pervades all the O'Dells on the desert clan side. Thelma was once again joined with Louise and I was ecstatic as the girl who gets to eat the last frosted rose on the birthday cake. Toni had spent that last six months in Firenze, Italia, studying none other than Italian, life and absorbing as much art as humanly possible. Our contact was limited to one phone call every two weeks on Sundays, five to ten minutes at twenty dollars, where I tried to hide my lamentations due to her absence. She had the next six months free before she left for school in New York and Texas was a stopping post to replenish the reserves and then figure out where she would travel onto next.

It was amazing having my favorite person on the planet down in my new favorite town and I lost no time showing her the shoe stores on Guadalupe and the thrift stores on South Congress. We replenished the art supplies and refueled the junk food tank, reserving all free time for art and Rice Krispie treats. I still had to work, the bane of being an adult, but would rush home at five to see what new craft had been invented. Picture frames, paintings, chalk drawings, journals, sculptures and jewelry were all born on the floor of our North Austin apartment and we soon designated a corner of the place for Toni 's workshop. As always does, boredom set in for the trailblazer and despite the job of bingo-calling we found for her at the retirement center, she decided she needed to go find something else to earn more money. Because of our location, the pickings were quite limited without a car. Both Viv and I had to be at work so early that we could not give her a ride unless her job directly coincided with our hours. The day she set out to look for work was the day she came back having already put seven hours on the time card. She could not help but lunge at me when I came home from the loan office with her exclamations of joy at having nailed the position as newest waitress at the IHOP across the street. I will admit I was astounded, which is another quality I have yet to shed my undying shock at every and all things despite their tendency to always happen. I'll never forget the day she told me she was going down to get a job at the cheekest shoe store back home. She was fifteen and completely inexperienced and walked back with her 'fifty- percent off' new employee discount card in hand two hours later. I warned Toni of the hard work that was in store for her at IHOP. She tended to align herself with jobs that were eternally fun and I had, on the other hand, the everlasting propensity to counteract her good luck with continual backbreaking employment.

"So how the hell did you land the job with no waitressing experience?" I asked.

"How can you ask such a thing? There were interviewing two other girls applying with experience, but I just wooed the manager with rapturous prophecies of how wonderful I was going to be that he hired me right away, not without telling me I had to take out my piercings though."

"Do you work tomorrow?"

"Yeah, it does kinda suck, but I work at seven every morning and supposedly get off at three, but you really get to go when you finish all your cleaning and all."

"So how much do you make an hour?" I asked.

"Something like, two an hour. I was kind of shocked, since I thought that everyone had to make at least minimum, but supposedly you claim your tips and tips are really good."

I became nervous that this job was gonna harden my little sister. I had seen some of the other women over at the Hop and was not about to have her coming home looking ragged. I figured how bad could a month be? She would be off traveling before that. "Well at least it's gonna be great experience for any other time you wanna waitress."

"That's exactly the point, and I can walk to work. I just need you to drive me to go and buy a uniform if that's cool."

"You guys havta pay for your own uniform?"

"Yeah, it's like twenty bucks or something. I figure I can find the poly pants at the Goodwill, but I need a red tie and then some white shirts. If you lose the pen that they give you, you havta pay six bucks to get a new one."

"They have a special pen?"

"Yeah, a magic pen, cool huh?"

I reveled in her ability to see good at the get go. We went and got her the necessary attire and I got up before seven to give her a ride on her first day. I only prayed that I would not be coming home to the defiled face of innocence.

After work, I was indeed met with the face of exhaustion. They had worked her over pretty good and yet she came out alive and kicking. I took a moment myself to peel off the office clothing of pretended conservatism and conformism and came back into the living room where Toni lay sprawled out on the couch watching the Wheel.

"So let's hear it," I told her.

Viv peered out from the laundry room and asked Toni to hold on until she finished separating her darks and lights. With a pile of dry towels in hand, she sat down on the floor and we prepared to hear the horrors of the first day.

"When I got inside and put my little apron on, the manager tells me that I'll be rotating with two other girls between register, hostess and juice girl, which I prefer to call the 'Juice Pusher.' So the register goes fine, I type in the amount, the cash button and about an hour goes by. As each person comes up to pay their bill, I smile and say, 'You guys have a nice weekend,' to which I proceed to get strange looks for which I have no comprehension why.

The girl who I am shadowing at the register says, 'Y'all sure have a good weekend,' in her thick Southern drawl to which she always gets a smile. After about forty-five minutes on the register, I am switched to the status of Juice Pusher, more commonly referred to as 'juice girl.' I pack my tray with four juices and set out to interrupt every happy diner by pushing our gross plastic bottled orange juice. The first half-hour went okay. Some wanted our juice, others did not and then we ran out of OJ. One of our managers showed me how to assemble a new one into the machine. As he finished, I filled up my tray and the manager made the motion of 'perfect, that's how you do it' and with one sweep of his hand smacked my tray into the air and flung the juice all over himself. I continuously apologized even though the sticky mess was totally inflicted by his own clumsiness."

"As it often is with men," I butt in and smile.

"After that, I got right back on target and went up one aisle where one of the servers, Jerry, says to me, 'You're doing good,' and just as I say 'thank you,' Linda runs into me and splatters each glass of juice all over the front of my shirt. So we clean that up and I set off again down another aisle. I find a table where one of the women in the corner of a group of four wants a juice and as I am pushing the juice across the table toward her, I forget about the other three juices still on my tray and they spill out onto the table and into the laps of the other customers. As all of this is going on, I think to myself, 'I will just have enough for the day to pay off the customers' dry-cleaning.'

In the distance, I can hear the other manager Mark saying to one of the waitresses, "Well Toni is just gonna have to watch where she's headed."

I say to myself, 'Fuck that! Sure I spilled the juice, but really only on two of the occasions had it been my fault.' At that point, I was hitting a valley in my nice atmosphere of plateaus. I could deal with my slips or spills, but the second that manager began to cap on me, well just screw him!"

"Screw him!" Viv agreed.

"Of course then Mark comes over, acting all nice and asks me, 'You doin' okay?'

And I say, 'Yeah, I'm doing great Mark, but I sure am better at register though.'

He says to me, 'You've got a good smile on, keep it up.'

I think of how much fun it would be to look into Mark's eyes and say with a smile, 'Being Juice Pusher sucks!'

As I walk down the same aisles with my tray, I begin chanting things in my head like, 'I'm gonna get ya, I'm gonna get ya.'

I think of walking up to tables and saying, 'Good morning folks! Would you like to start your day off with a refreshing glass of orange juice?' and then when they very politely reply, 'No thank you,' I could scream, 'TAKE THE FUCKING JUICE OR I'LL SPILL IT ALL OVER YOU!'

Luckily these thoughts just enable me to keep up my smile and live vicariously through the wanderings of my mind."

"You poor thing," I say as I give her a hug.

"Did you make any tips?" Viv asks with condolence.

"No, we don't get tips while we shadow, plus I wasn't kidding about the dry-cleaning. Two of the women asked it taken out of my wages," Toni says.

"That is just down-right mean," Viv says.

"Well, it can't be any worse tomorrow. I'm sure that was just the flounders of a first day," Toni says with weariness. She falls asleep right after dinner and her 'juice pushing' days come to an end when IHOP outlaws the trial experience after about four days. For the first couple weeks she came home with fifty to sixty bucks a day in tips and near the end of her waitressing experience she pulled down an easy hundred a day and even more on weekends.

Austin was hardly limited to all work and no play for Toni though. She did have to work weekends, so I volunteered extra hours at the retirement facility, where Viv essentially lived. Her, Viv, and I got used to the hours easily enough to begin bowling in the evenings and taking in a plethora of movies. Some nights were just devoted solely to the craft corner, hair dying, cutting and eyebrow plucking. A week did not pass by without a visit to the Highlife, one of our favorite cafes for enormous mochas and humus that did not satisfy Vivian's particular Middle Eastern pallet, but did the trick for Toni and I. Toni quit her career as a waitress about a week before the music festival, not without making friends with the resident speed-freaking customers and one marriage proposal from an illegal alien vowing to take up the smallest amount of space in our closet after the trip to City Hall.

It is sometimes difficult to remember how those weeks flourished so fast and what exactly we did to pass the little time we had holding onto one address, but most of all it was about talking. It was about creating and painting, sketching portraits of one another, and staying up late in bed just philosophizing about our impending fame, genetics, nature versus nurture, planning when we'd move to London and when my eyebrows might grow back. For all the years

I used to wonder if one of us was adopted, we then pondered the potentiality of Mom freezing my split egg and baring it four years and eleven months later. One night I went to bed, listening to a Tom Waits tape and we found ourselves that next night sleeping on Canal Street during a thunderous rain storm with the sound of the Riverboats moaning down the Mississippi.

The next morning, we got up, jumped in the car and hauled ass across Texas and into Louisiana. That week in New Orleans, I accidentally loaded the camera with nothing but black and white film and kicked myself later for thirty-six pictures that held such color in our minds and yet nothing but various shades of gray on paper. It was still unforgettable. We walked in the hard rain, ate soggy pizza and imagined Toni's work hanging in one of the small galleries down Royale. I pointed out the patio I wished to claim as my own and we ate grits and eggs and hashbrowns for less than two fifty each while flirting with waiters with Cajun accents and gazing from windows of dripping ivy. I thought I saw a witch. We spent an afternoon baiting two dogs the size of buffaloes through a gate yard until the owner scolded us and we made a run for Saint Louis Cathedral. An entire morning was spent laying on the peeling green painted benches in the square of the church, across from the Mississippi where we did nothing more than lick the sugar from our hands which held three pastries each. We stared up at the sky, calling out cloud shapes and paralleling them to Hollywood movie stars.

We stayed in a four star hotel, watching HBO when the rain really began to pour down and our socks were too wet to go back out in. Polishing off a loaf of bread each and a jar of peanut butter from the five and dime across the street, we imagined living in fancy hotels for the rest of our lives, a dream that was only countered by the romantic possibilities of exploring all the youth hostels and their inhabitants in Europe. We spoke of what made us happy and wholeheartedly agreed that the top of the list was family, not forgetting how Mom had always told us we were each other's family in the end. A stroll through the river market, grapes, plums and cheap sunglasses later found us driving back across the highway stretching out over the water, the water that magically covered the roots of all the trees, trees that looked like ghosts or pictures snapped and frozen among a black and white world. The storm of thunder and lightning washed us home, home to Austin, a home we had in common for a little more than a month.

We arrived back from the dream and *South by Southwest* remained just a day away. Viv and I continued to work through the week and Toni amused our friend Kasey, who had flown in for the festival. Our nights were rushed, fun I should say, more good times were pushed into those five days than I will hardly be able to remember. We went to the opera, saw four independent films and almost thirty bands. Outside *Stubb's Barbeque* the first night we waited to be let inside and then found spots on the side stage to sit and huddle together in the cold.

"It is *so* freezing!" Kasey squealed as she sat in her full-length sailor's pea coat and thick socks.

I ran my hand up and down Toni's back in rapid motion to prevent her from freezing. "You must be dying," I whispered as I looked down at her sandals, short skirt and thin sweater.

"I'm not so bad," she smiled through bluish lips, "I'm just having so much fun!"

Vivian smiled over as her own left set of toes attempted to cover the right ones and laughed at Toni's positivity so reminiscent to me, of her own. We didn't get home that night until well after four in the morning and still we stayed up and talked in bed until I had to get up for work at six. Sometimes it isn't until the end, that you see your time together so fleeting and yet it was never unappreciated. Toni still talks of the electric green fiddle played by *Imani Coppola* and the blue glitter wig she wore that night, *Soul Asylum*'s lead guitarist and the vampiric face on those *Flick* brothers. That voice of a little girl that echoed out of the youngest boy's mouth remains haunting even to this day.

It wasn't really our first *South by Southwest* for which I will remember Toni 's visit out to Austin. It might have been less fun without her and yet it is the trips to the Chinese Buffet Palace that stick to the edges of my mind, the only time I could be outnumbered on quantity of pork bows digested in one sitting. It was the way she'd offer to make S'mores when I came home from work and insisted upon the fact that she would not consume a nuked Rice Krispie treat, to which she so convinced Vivian that the microwave is used for little other than popcorn now. Drawing pictures, drinking coffee at Jim's, watching old movies, and trips to the thrift stores were more fun than any concert, opera or film festival with Toni.

I knew it was time for her to leave when I sensed her becoming too comfortable, a concept I can convince myself exists, but will probably never sift through my version of life. I knew when the music was over, Kasey had left and the Academy Awards had come and gone (an event that can never be shared with anyone more understanding of its importance than my mother and of course Toni). I knew when I overheard her discussing potential plans of traveling the country by train and then deciding instead upon trekking up to Seattle for a few months before heading off to her already aligned summer job down in the Florida Keys, that it was time for my sister to fly away.

When I shuddered that last morning as the toast jumped out of the toaster, perfectly timed, the same minute of each morning of every day, Toni asked me, "What are you so afraid of George?"

And I answered her. "I don't know. I really don't know."

However, I *do* know. I'm afraid that I do not know how to be fearless, how to exist without the crutch of abandoned safety. I do not yet know how to make it to New Orleans on my own, even though it is me who drove, without the map, along the 10 with no turns. I do know that the chaos from which I tried to shelter my angel sister is only an illusion, for one cannot keep the truth hidden from anyone with half a brain for so long. I know that she who knows the truth and does not allow herself to become enslaved is more than just a girl who is pretending to be innocent. She is more than Peter Pan, she is the girl in the snow suit, all grown up at the top of the mountain, sailing past the Ponte Vecchio with the truth as her armor and cynicism cast to the wind. Nevertheless, it is there, the danger and the sense of realism dripping over her ideals like paper covers rock. It is there, wanting to lash out at her, spoil her, strip her of her angel's wings, but she is better than a child, smarter than a seraph because she has met it, walked with it, is best friend's with it. The danger, the cynicism and that, which spoils, resides in me and as long as she loves them, she must not be afraid. As long as I wrestle with reality and forbid it to nail down her wings, she can fly, and away she does. She flies off to the Keys, off to Seattle, back again to Europe and then New York. She flies away, my little snow girl, one of those O'Dell sisters, conquering the world, an avalanche falling from the mountain, covering the Earth with a little more idealism and the notion that some of us never have to grow up.

Saying it Out Loud

We sit in traffic and Vivian looks sad. She said goodbye to her boyfriend today, who is her best friend, but no longer her lover. We arrive at the Cineplex halfway through the previews. The movie proves to be too long, but some of the things the actors said spoke to me. I may have to read the book. Anything Robert Redford says sounds important. "It was not difficult to see that it was over. It was saying it out loud that was almost impossible." He looked defeated when he said that, much the same way Vivian does right now. He was paid to look that way. Vivian senses that what she said was never important to him, her boyfriend I mean.

After the movie we sat outside the Continental Club. Vivian wanted to go inside. I was too tired and said, "We should sit in the car and sleep a little first."

She watched the men walking down south Congress. None of them were very attractive, but nobody appears to be after staring at Robert Redford's perfectly weathered mug for three hours. Vivian thinks the men are going to watch us while we sleep. I know that when I see people in cars, I never stare. I am in fact, always leery. Viv laughs at that, sadly though. She seems comforted that people will *know* that we are strange.

I lose my keys while I am sleeping. Viv says that she is sure I am sitting on them. She is correct. I close the door, step up onto the curb and into a crevice in the sidewalk. My chartreuse platform sandals flip sideways and I lay sprawled out onto the cement. Vivian leans on her knees and nearly busts her gut laughing. There is no detection of sadness in her smile, this time. I pick the pebbles out of my knee and look to see if anyone else has been resting in their cars.

Everyone is inside and the show has started. Kathy is drunk and dedicates every one of her songs to Jon Dee. I am a little embarrassed. He is at the bar smoking an American Spirit, sipping his whiskey. People do that here, sip their whiskey. It is very different from California and the movies, where they slug their shots or drink from thin blue straws with little umbrellas that never hit their noses.

I think I could love Jon Dee. Everyone in the Continental already knows that Kathy does. He sounds a little like Joe Cocker and like Tom Waits to me. He sings about how he does not want to be faithless - Jon Dee, not Tom Waits. Everybody knows Tom already lost his faith. His voice is like what it must be like to gargle with shards of glass. It makes him beautiful, that voice. It makes him more real than Robert Redford, and some women need that. I believe that I am one of them.

We slip away after a couple of hours. Both Vivian and I were falling asleep anyway. I tell her how we should come back next Wednesday with my little tape recorder. It wouldn't be wrong because I already bought his CD. We probably will not do it anyway. There is not much time left. I feel it pressing on me, the little time left that is.

Sitting in traffic on 35 going home, Vivian looks through the pictures and again tells me how she genuinely loves the one of me exposing my drooping chin. At least there are wildflowers in it and a big cloudy sky. I might grow to like it. Certainly after we are gone and everything ever horrible becomes a memory of something fabulous, I will probably love it. But then again, there has not been anything horrible, except maybe this day for Vivian.

I do believe that it is the fast pace that Vivian insists on running her life that may have left her best friend behind. Then again, he never really tried to run along with her. In fact, I think that he would not have found such significance in Jon Dee's voice, Kathy's drunken dedications, or resting in the car for an hour. I do not think he would have let it go unsaid when we stopped at DQ for the second time that day or when I asked Vivian to take my picture kneeling down in front of that grave in Waco (which she might have even found sacrilegious, but did it fast anyway).

Vivian told me that it is those things that she holds onto so tightly. Even though she can't remember the names and people or the names of the places. (I mean she really does not retain them at all) she searches for them - the experiences. She runs into them at MACH speed, fleeing the stagnancy of what she knows, away from all sense of safety, which even freaks me out (although I pretend that it does not). Maybe if he would have pretended, it would have lasted...a few more months. But "I do not know," which is something I am shocked I put on paper for prosperity. I *do* know that I am upset with myself for liking that one droning country song, but it plays on the radio incessantly, mocking me. It's Johnny and I forgive my taste for knowing every word.

"I fell into a burning ring of fire. I went down, down, down, and the flames went higher. And it burns, burns, burns, the ring of fire, the ring of fire..."

I wonder where the accident may be because we have not moved. Vivian will not fall asleep because I know that secretly, she is afraid of my driving. Okay, maybe not secretly. Maybe someday she will not be so sad. This year was supposed to be our year of transition. I believe this year was already fated. I have already done my transforming and Vivian never thinks that she changes, which she may not feel tomorrow. I know that she will not allow herself to remain so sad.

There is too much to do before we leave. There's that waiter at the High Life Café with the blue eyes and the almost black hair. Who knows? Maybe he's not gay. Tomorrow there's always the Electric Lounge. Viv wants to see that angel movie. There is still half a roll of black and white film in the camera, more sky, more wildflowers, a country full of DQ's, more grizzled voices who will remind us that it is not time to

be faithless and even when we know it, they will say it
out loud.

Mel McCabe

Candy, Kasey & the Congo

It's hard to say just when your childhood friends take on the title 'childhood' friends and not just simply friends, although with Kasey and I, our friendship did begin when we were only eleven. Oh, to think of that first meeting, back on the first day of sixth grade when she walked up to me and uttered the words that only a transplant from the city, friendless and fresh to the Peninsula could utter, "Can I come over to your house today?" It was a friendship born of necessity and one day later grown into a kindred. Never have I met someone with whom I would have more in common than Kasey. Although, it is difficult to decipher which parts of each other were alike before we met and when one might have become so much like the other as we molded each other into adults, out of the twenty-three and a half hour a day exposure. It was the kind of

67

friendship that began when we were only eleven and did not end until it was time for us to part ways and leave me waving goodbye to the van at the end of Burnett Avenue heading on up to a new life at Humboldt State College. The fates that sundered the kindred brought them back together two years later, destined, as it would seem, to never part. Never came sooner than both of us projected though and after graduation from our respective schools on either side of the Bay it came time again to part ways. This time it would be Kasey who stood at the end of the Avenue waving goodbye to the packed car, this time set for further destination and who knew, but for a longer time.

The initial trip out to Austin was not made without my best friend, although the town did not haunt her, or find its way under her skin in quite the same way it squirmed its charm beneath mine. At the restaurant near the record store back home I asked her, "Are you coming or what? I really think that we'd have a great time and I know Viv would love it too."

My pleas were heard on deaf ears and our paths were not set to run parallel into our twenties. Our lives diverged and the friendship, I suppose then turned into what one may deem a 'childhood' one, although she still remains the closest thing I'll ever have to a second sister. Phone calls were cut to the quick on my end of the cord and I began my life down in Texas with the resolution to enter upon everything anew, including friendships. This hollowed determination was seen by me for just that, quite unfilled by the end of a good four months and one phone call later when Kasey bought a ticket to come out and visit (coincidentally on the most ideally popular weekend of Austin, *South by Southwest* Music Festival).

It often proves difficult when one gets time off work for vacationing and the vistee is unable to take the same time off work as well. The way in which I was operating at the time was quite hand to mouth, working for a temporary agency that basically yelled, 'jump' as I screamed 'how high?' Any free time was usually put in at the retirement house across the street, washing dishes and slinging grits and pancakes. To make it sound as though it was not fun or was done out of necessity should not be implied. I knew, as well as my folks, that corporate America lay only one door knocking away and physical labor and mundane tasks were merely my *own* choice at a plot to save my soul from forgetting its artistic passions. The philosophy for me was self-deemed down in Texas, 'Find yourself comfortable and run the risk of stagnancy.'

Toni and Vivian shared my understanding. Although Viv was at the retirement center in a capacity that ran closer to her final medical destination, 'med-supeing' was more about a year of play for my 'cousin,' than working for the words to print on the resume. Toni backed me up in my endeavors of the heart with the way in which only a little sister formulating her own life in five years could. I believe that Kasey too, understood my need to 'just get by' in quite a different way though. Kasey remained as many of us in our early twenties, still searching for the fuel to make her soul zoom. The honest truth was that I knew (in a way I am not quite sure that she had figured out) that Kasey's desires lay in so many pieces to 'the puzzle' that she needed only to pick one to find it all fitting together. For that third week in March, Kasey had caught a slight spell of the downtrodden heebee geebees, and the friend who might have appeared to have abandoned her in her hour of sadness was probably not the right one to cure the sickness. Luckily, Toni had a way of, maybe not curing, yet indeed making people forget.

I got home the first night of Kasey's visit and found that she and Toni had spent much of the day wandering Guadalupe, finding the vegetarian restaurant on the corner where they had actually spotted Paul Mitchell.

"Oh, George, you woulda freaked. It was so classic for me to come out here and see someone famous, in Austin of all places. Toni and I were stuffing our faces on chow-mien and tofu and who walks in, but Paul. I told Toni to pull her hair the hell outta that pony tail holder and begin thrashing it about in those shampoo commercial sort of ways, but the freak was blind. The chick with him had nappy hair to boot," Kasey said in one breath without any need for a comma.

I cast my memory back to the first time my mother had heard Kasey talk and thought it fabulous that I had managed to land myself a foreign exchange student as my new best friend. And to think it had all began as she had walked up to me in those scary whitewashed halls of sixth grade to so boldly ask, "Can I come over to your house today?" Two weeks later my mother had begun to learn the talk of 'the Valley' and only had to beg both of us as little as maybe two, three times a day to pause in between sentences. Listening once again to my old accent, caused me to remember the incessant razzing I received for what was first thought of as a speech impediment in my move to Chicago and then believed to be the drawl of none other than a city-slicker amongst the non-transient Austinites. It seemed as though I had almost abandoned my affectation to the Valley as we whizzed on past the Santa Ana on our journey out until it quickly leapt to the back of my throat after five minutes with Kasey.

I set Kasey up on the inflatable air mattress in the 'guest room,' which might have been used as a dining room for other inhabitants of Keystone Apartments who owned kitchen tables and chairs. She threw her bags and shoes at the foot of the bed in the fashion I had forgotten taught Toni how to be 'creatively' messy and we all set out for the local Mexican restaurant.

"You guys aren't happy that I'm here, are you? Did I come at a bad time or did I do something to piss you off?" Kasey asked after the waitress had placed my water in front of me and I began to squeeze the lemon onto the cubes with a smile.

I glanced over at Vivian with an unintentional look of shock, which probably did not add justification to the negation, "I don't know what you're talkin' about Kasey. Of course I wanted you to come out. I asked you to come, didn't I?"

"Yeah, I know, maybe I just sound paranoid, but I just don't feel welcome," she retorted.

I didn't know how else to back up my defense. I had taken half a day off of work to pick her up from the airport, thrown my arms around her as she stepped off the plane and was sitting across from her at the dinner table. This was the only other time I had seen her since she had arrived the afternoon before. Was that it? Me sitting next to Viv? I did not know how to play *the game* anymore. Was it the inflatable bed? The comment I had made about the pile of thrown clothes? Maybe I was unintentionally giving off a vibe. Maybe Viv and I had been living together so long that we didn't know how to interact with other humans? Whatever it was, I'd deny it, hell my subconscious was already doing so.

We survived the next few days with much of the same tension present in the first. Neither Kasey nor I wanted to say what was wrong. I think that I truly had little idea as to what lay at the root of the problem. I had taught Kasey the art of never confronting anyone, or maybe she taught me, we'll never know, but the issue probably had much to do with the distance that had sprouted between us and the inability to fit together in quite the same way we used to. Each of us still had the same habits, both needed one entire pot of coffee in the morning just to eek out more than a yawn. We each watched *Entertainment Tonight* as if it still remained the only hardcore news show on television, lived for hair-band reunions, admitted that fact to no one, and could not go more than three weeks without changing *our* hair color, weeding out our closets and fleeing to none other than the nearest thrift store for replenishment. The difference now was that we did not do these things together. Kasey and I were still alike, as much the same as when people used to confuse one for the other (even though we looked nothing alike) back in our old high school halls and yet our lives were being lived further apart than we had ever been. It probably was me, me who cut the umbilical cord that afternoon I drove off down the driveway, eastward in the direction of my new life, but I had not intended to cause the pain. I believe that it was I, who first felt wounded in fact.

We stood in my parents' kitchen, saying our goodbyes through veiled vision and rivers of tears when Kasey said, "This is gonna be good for you George. You go out there and bust a move. Don't pull any of that fear crap. This is gonna be *sooo* good for you."

Once said, the well of tears dried up. I jumped in my car and floored it all the way to Tucson with no regrets for leaving, with less than a shred of despondency for my best friend being left behind. Maybe it was rancorous, maybe it was hardened and downright mean of me not to forgive such a comment made in great dejection and yet I could not wipe the tone of condescension that accompanied the words. Maybe I had been apprehensive. Maybe moving out to Austin *was* a 'good thing for me,' and yet I did not want the sagacious words that were supposed to erupt from only the mouth of one's mother to come out of the best friend who had decided not come with me, the friend whom I felt had little reason to be informing me what was good for me when I would never have thought to speculate on the morality of another, her, or anyone. I believe that was the moment we became *childhood* friends, maybe that was when I became far less afraid and more armored in my war against the world, the one in which I was gonna come out victorious, successful and dream fulfilled. Whatever the analogy, whatever the grudge that had been kept, I felt little ire remained that March week of *South by Southwest*. All that really might have shown through then, was a small feeling of culpability. I somehow felt guilty for loving my life and somehow sad that I sensed Kasey did not love hers. For this, there was really nothing I could do.

The next two nights were fun-filled. It would have been difficult to not have a good time when a city offers seven hundred bands, at fifty different clubs, all for the admission of one sixty-dollar wristband. It became Vivian's and my mission to see as many distinct bands as possible and make it into the inside of as many different clubs as well. Our days of our hermit lifestyles were promised to end at the beginning of the festival and our favorite clubs were indeed discovered among those first few nights and well into the hours of many mornings. Work proved the shackles that bound the two of us to our human existence despite the superhuman powers that had us dragging the two that were able to sleep in every morning from one end of Sixth Street to the other, from seven in the evening until five in the morning. I had done my part in organizing the week, by sifting through the hundreds of band names and planning the itinerary according to my perceived tastes of the four players in our troupe. The paper was left on the coffee table all day, every day, so that while I punched away the hours on the work clock, a change in schedule could be made with little argument from me, if the other party so desired to see a different band or go to another venue. No changes were made and we clung hard to the white sheet of paper which remained always folded in my back jeans pocket, to become more tattered by Saturday night. If a band was put on the list, it was seen and heard. We did not intent to play the parts of weaklings; we were taking our first festival by storm.

Standing in line outside La Zona Rosa for the *Spacehog* show, we thanked the gods that we didn't have to spend the evening in the cold as the previous night at *Stubb's*. I had never in any of my Christmas's in the snow or Midwestern winter school days heard such clamoring grief over the cold as erupted from the lips of Kasey that night. Most ironically were the facts that as Kasey sat on the club's outdoor wooden deck adorned in her woolen pea coat and socks, Viv pulled at the edges of her short shorts and Toni rubbed her blue toes peeping out from thong flip-flops. As I wondered why I myself had worn a short skirt, all that ended Kasey's complaints of the chill were new one's directed towards why I was hugging my frail and scantily clad sister when I should have been wondering about her (my friend in the woolen clothes)! We swapped the negative complaints on Friday night for fresh problems on Saturday, the irreparable damage of our shattered ear-dreams. And oh man, did our ears take a beating as we all found it necessary to purchase earplugs for no less than six bucks a pop just to make it through the second act. After *Bran Van,* we slumped down against the cement wall and rested our legs as well as our ears. As Toni spoke of some radio station back in the Bay Area, Viv leaned in to hear through the equipment check and Kasey's concentration drifted off to the guy in the corner wearing a red pizza jacket. I watched her giving him the eye and focused back on Toni before I saw him walk over and sit down next to Kasey. Vivian looked over at me and I sensed that Kasey seemed a bit uncomfortable. I motioned for Toni to turn toward Kasey and her new friend and we gathered around to listen to their conversation.

"So, as I was saying," the guy shouted, "My sister and I come to the festival every year, but this time she told me that I can't hang out with her anymore."

I caught Viv's eye in the corner of mine and a strange vibe was confirmed. Kasey gave the guy a compassionate smile and put her hand on his, and said, "That is so rude! I cannot believe your sister! Well, I'm glad you found us."

"So what's your name?" my overtly friendly sibling shouted over the speaker.

"Candelero Antonia, but my friends call me Candy," he bellowed back through a wide-toothed grin.

"What's your astrological sign?" Kasey inquired as I turned to roll my eyes upon hearing a line I thought had been shot in 1983.

"I'm a Cancer," Candy said with a smile unparalleled to that of Jack Nickelson's in *The Shining*, "I was born on July 10th."

Kasey spun around and grabbed my hand, "George! Did you hear that? Candy has the same birthday as you. And Toni his last name is the same as yours!" She turned back to Candy and explained that Toni's name was a nickname for Antonia.

"Wowzers! Meeting you all must have been meant to be!" Candy shouted out as I managed to shoot Kasey a less than thankful glance for finding commonality between my sister, this very strange man and me.

"So where is your sister?" Kasey questions, "Are you staying with her?"

I waited for the point in the conversation where Kasey would begin to feel so bad for this stranger that she'd invite him back to our apartment for the evening. "Well, she says I'm a psycho and that she can't meet people when she's around me," Candy stated.

I began to wonder why this man was so forward with his unappealing personal information. A strange vibe was more than apparent. Kasey smiled over at me and Candy continued to speak in an effort to divert her attention back at him, "I am schizophrenic and I do have violent tendencies and my sister told me that I need to let everyone know that before you let me go anywhere with you because she said it would be wrong to lie to you. Does that bother you?"

I immediately scanned the room for the bouncer and other large men who might be good matches for Candy if these tendencies began to rear their ugly heads. My eyes caught on Viv and Toni's as they had widened to flying saucer status. Kasey leaned in a little closer to me while giving Candy a reassuring smile that said, "Please do not hurt us."

Vivian took the opportunity to tell Candy that all four of us needed to go to the bathroom. We got up from the floor and beat feet to the bathroom, clinging hard to the concept of separate sex facilities in times when just about everything else was modernizing.

"Kasey, what the hell are you doing, picking up crazy people like that?" I screamed as the door shut behind us and we found ourselves alone with thirty-two other women in line, fighting for a spot to reapply make-up at the mirror.

Kasey looked from one of our faces to the next with her own face of panic, "I don't mean to attract the freaks. They just flock to me as though I were their weekend asylum."

"Oh please!" Toni cried out, "I saw that one for the loon he is, a mile away!"

"Oh, that is *so* not true. You guys are just judgmental bitches!" Kasey shouted out in defense.

"Okay, we're not gonna get nasty here," Vivian, 'the voice of reason' protested. "I will admit that the guy seemed a little strange to me from the get go, but now that we know he is demented let's not fight over who saw it first and rather spend our short bout in the bathroom as a time to assess just how to lose him."

I glanced down at Viv and in protest whispered in Kasey's direction, "I may be a bitch, but at least I don't put the rest of us in danger. I was just waiting for you to invite him back home."

"Please," Kasey said with rolled eyes, "He's really not *that* bad of a guy."

"Kasey!" Toni shouted, "The guy admitted to no less than having violent tendencies, not even suicidal ones, murderous ones, like the 'slit ya in the back while you're grovin' to *Fastball*' in five minutes! This is not really very funny."

I took that opportunity to let out a nervous snicker because it really was funny, funny that we were in the situation, an event taking place that seemed ludicrous and then again quite normal when you put us all together.

"Okay, okay," Vivian spoke in a calming demeanor, "We need to just go back out there and stick to the front of the stage, blend and maybe he'll get the hint."

We all tromped back out of the bathroom as though one could imagine us all pissing at the same time, wiping, pulling up our pants and flinging the stalls open in unison to a Sister Sledge tune. We squirmed our way to the front of the crowd to find none other than Candelero right at the stage, watching us, particularly Kasey as we all filed into the crowd.

"I was wonderin' where y'all were. This is great, huh?" Candy questioned.

I ignored Kasey's pleading, 'save me' expression and directed my eyes toward the stage above her head where I had resigned my thinking to, 'hell, he seems to like Kasey, not necessarily the rest of us,' as I waited for the band to come out. After *Fastball*, we headed over to the wall in wait for the next band to finish setting up.

"You guys know that I live near the green river?" Candy commented.

"The green river?" I asked like a dumbshit for even paying attention.

"Yeah," Candy continued, still staring at Kasey, "In San Antonio, for Saint Patrick's day weekend, they dye the whole river green."

I doubted the validity of the statement. I mean, how the hell did one go about changing the color of an entire river for a few days, but I did not see the harm in letting the man's imagination wander, better than to anger him.

All but Kasey had lost their patience for Candy and begun to feel less sympathy for Kasey since she had invited the man to hang out with us in the first place. Kasey continued to lean in closer to me whenever Candy would begin to ask her what she wanted to do after each band finished their set or when he would try to again obtain her phone number, *our* phone number. After *Spacehog* and one very violent mosh pit that

Toni did not have the novelty of claiming she escaped without a few major bruises, we filed out of the building and headed back to the car. Toni and I walked arm and arm singing *Mambo City* as we stared at one another out of the corner of our eyes unknowingly wondering how to lose Candy. As we turned onto Lavaca nothing was left to ponder as Candy instinctively grabbed Kasey's right thigh with both his arms, causing her to trip. Kasey screamed as she smacked her chin against the pavement and landed on her face. Candy landed on top of Kasey and Toni and I each seized an arm and began to hoist half of Candy's body up from Kasey, still face down on the sidewalk. Vivian lifted her leg and kicked Candy squarely in the face. Unsure as to whether or not Candy had been fully affected, Viv lifted her leg again (unfortunately at the same time Kasey chose to lift her head up from the pavement) and planted her tennis shoe directly into Kasey's forehead. Candy's nose had begun to bleed as he lay back down on top of Kasey. Leaving no time for Kasey to react, Viv, Toni and I yanked her out from underneath Candelero and managed to book it full-throttle to the Daihatsu, our tiny den of safety for the night.

We ended up at Jim's. Their four o'clock crowd on a weekend, other than *South by Southwest*, has the tendency to run the risk of reminding one a lot of Candelero Antonia. I recall how badly Vivian had just wanted to go home and crawl into bed on that last night of the festival. Four in the morning hurts when you've only had an hour of sleep each night for the past five days and gone on to work doubles at five thirty a.m. on the med pass. Somehow mornings are supposed to ache in your twenties though, sometimes anyway. That morning in the coffee shop, Kasey went to the bathroom to nurse the already forming golf ball-size bump on her forehead. It was easy to see that we were all a little irritated at the situation, a little clouded by the possibility of being killed and a little more than weary. I tried to convince the other two in our booth that it would all just be a faded minute memory of the festival in less than a year. Yet it has been longer than that and I still recall it like the all-out alley brawl it was, this very second. Kasey returned from the ladies room and said to us all, "I had the best time here. I really love this town and this festival."

Vivian had passed the breaking point, a point I did not believe she even possessed and retorted, "Really? I didn't think you had a good time at all?" Toni looked over at me with a face of surprise. For me though, recalling the complaints of the cold, the anger in how she had not felt welcome at our intro dinner, followed by the panic in her evening still continuing on into that morning, I could not throw a surprised look upon my mug. I was too tired to pretend.

"You guys really think I'm a complainer, huh?"

Viv answered before we could, "Yeah, it seems that way."

"I think you just show happiness differently Kasey" I poured out over the earlier lamentation.

"Well, I *did* have a good time, I really did. I'm sorry if you don't think so," Kasey explained.

Old friends die hard, a saying that meant nothing to me a year ago, now echoes within the corridors of my head. We used to have this knit purple gypsy fortuneteller hat with a pearl and rhinestone quarter moon on the front that my sister and I would fight over when we were kids. I remember my mother had a mint green one that she wore as a legitimate fashion statement in the seventies, if any article of clothing can be deemed legitimate from that decade today. Toni would put it on and beg me to fix her red lipstick so that she looked less like Punchy the Clown and more like Madame Zelda.

"Just why are you making this such a big deal Toni? The lipstick looks fine, now can *I* wear the hat?" I pleaded; smart enough to know if I simply pried it off her head she would scream.

"I am not Toni. I am Zelda," she said her in best six-year-old attempt at the Greek accent, "I am the Queen gypsy fortuneteller from the school of Detroit Magic."

"Detroit Magic?" I questioned with great nerve and eyes rolled as far toward the crown of my forehead as humanly possible. "Just what can Madame Zelda tell me about my future?" I asked with little enthusiasm and much desire to put the hat on myself.

"Zelda believes you to be thirsty. You need to drink child, you must avoid the phone, pay more attention to Zelda and remember everyone has one story. There is a story for everyone…"

To most, Queen Zelda allegorizes the need to ignore melodramatic children. At the age of ten and a half, to me, she was nothing more than a royal pain in the ass, an ignoramus and the reason I sometimes paid our next-door neighbor to play with her so that I would no longer be obligated. Upon turning twelve though, when I was no longer *thirsty* and in fact often drunk and at eighteen when the failure to take stock in the premonitions to avoid the phone left me and my car wrapped around a telephone pole, I began to believe in the melodrama of one small child and was anxious to decipher the riddle of everyone having a story. 'One story,' Madame Zelda had said. *'There is one story for everyone.'*

I am not so superstitious and thickheaded, to ignore that six-year-old Toni probably wanted me to get her a glass of milk that day of the prophecy and at the same time she tried to make me believe that I was thirsty. She wanted me to pay her more attention than the friends with whom I had just begun to obsessively converse with on the phone at the ripe old age of ten. As far as the 'one story,' I really do believe we were dealing with a highly intelligent child who knew of what she spoke. Most likely, others will remember us each as characters in a story, clinging to their memory as it struggles to remain attached to our fading faces. It is probable that Toni really did too have a gift. I mean hell, we *are* half Bedouin, that's Gypsy in some languages, soothsayers, fortunetellers, storytellers, magic makers, writers...That is Toni's story for which I will always recollect her, the fortuneteller and of course the flying snow bunny of yesteryear. But that's another story. This is Kasey's.

We weren't any older than thirteen. I wish I could say now that we were even younger for the immaturity to which it took to carry out this act of innocence, but we were indeed thirteen, naïve and believing we wanted to live the lives of spies on the brink of danger. We sat in the back of Ed's army green van and reveled at the coolness of Kasey's Mom and step-dad. They actually liked *U2's* 'Joshua Tree', which we thought to be evidence of the voice of angels singing. Both sides had played twice before we made it up to my folks' cabin, where we intended on swimming 'til our fingers turned to raisins and sunbathing 'til our bodies turned the color of the very heart of a watermelon. Nora and Ed dropped us off at the lodge in the evening so that we could play bingo and they could try and catch the 49er game at a bar in town. Bingo proved rather dull and so we abandoned the stakes of free ice cream winnings and walked down to the lake to scope out the young teenage guys. Where we found few strapping young men, we did encounter a plethora of bats, one in fact strapping itself to my face, whereupon I had to shake it free within my jacket as I feared screaming so loud I might cause reason for the fire department to become alarmed. It didn't take longer than half a second after the bat extracted itself from my face to abandon the lake and head back up to the pool area where they were still calling Bingo numbers.

"I'm famished," Kasey declared when we had reached the top of the hill. "Let's go up to the snack bar and get some food. Ed and my Mom gave us money for whatever we want."

I had to admit I was pretty damn hungry. I don't think either of us had eaten all day and a day in the sun and in the water tends to really work up your appetite. By the time we made it to the snack bar, we could have eaten at least three hot dogs and a good helping of nachos each. Wouldn't you guess, the snack bar was closed for the night. Ed and Nora were not coming back from the game for at least three hours. We were stranded at the lodge, four miles downhill from the cabin and starving. Thirty minutes later the possibilities had narrowed to only one, we were walking back to the cabin, all either of us could think about was the mint chip ice cream in the freezer and the leftover baked chicken in the fridge. Walking through town would have lessened the journey by a mile. We figured though, that if Ed and Nora saw us walking past the bar, they would think we were both rather unintelligent in our plight and being dangerous as seventh graders trekking along the side of the highway with no lights and only townie trucks passing in the night. So off we ventured past the lake, past the other lake and all the way up Nola Drive, hiking like we'd never see the cabin before the light of day. Before we reached the halfway mark, it dawned on us that we would realistically only be able to stay at the cabin for a few moments to gorge upon provisions before we'd have to run at light-speed back to the lodge if Ed and Nora were gonna get there right after the game. The last thing we wanted was to be thought of as two of the lost children of the night. I mean it *was* Skull's County in which we were running loose. Reaching the cabin proved incredibly and shockingly anticlimactic. All most people really want to do after having hiked four miles at a damn good clip is rest. We each ate about three spoonfuls of ice cream, one wing on the hen and were headed back down the hill, this time through town with the hope that we would possibly get there before the parentals, with the mile shaved off the return trip. As we progressed through town, we both hunched down past the two bars, not knowing which one Ed and Nora had settled upon, and then walked quickly up the highway in the hull of the ditch at the side of the road. I had to continue to remind Kasey not too get to close to the edge of the highway for fear that passing semis would not spot us, as they rolled by going seventy-five miles an hour, hauling ass up Highway 4. As the trucks began to get louder and the passengers more vocal, I began to grow more angry and irritated that the lodge turn-off was much further from the outskirts of town than I had expected.

"I'm tired George! It's getting cold. I think we're lost. Are we lost? I'm so tired!" Kasey complained.

"Pull you hair back Kasey and look more like a man!" I shouted a few feet behind, feeling much the same way as she and yet not prepared to share the negativity out loud as getting back to the lodge in one piece was the highest priority.

"Well I thought you said that the turn off was just up ahead. We've been walking for more than forty-five minutes now and I think we passed it."

That thought hadn't escaped my imagination either, but I didn't wanna hear it out loud so I merely snapped, "I think we should just take a ride with the next truck that passes."

"Are you kidding me?" Kasey looked back with a look of sheer horror and the drilled mind of McGruff the crime fighter screaming out at my impending poor judgment.

A truck pulled off the road as I was getting ready to argue and I walked toward the back of it just as the twenty-one-year-old male in the passenger seat thrust a dead chicken in my face, forcing me to tumble back into the ditch. He and the driver squealed with laughter as they peeled off, tossing up the dirt from their tires.

I began to cry as Kasey took one look at me and could not help but laugh. "Oh, I think you should have jumped in the back of that one! Yep, if that wasn't divine intervention, I don't know what is," Kasey shouted out.

Before either one of us was able to kill the other, we made it back to the lodge. It took us another good hour and the idea of sleeping in the ditch for pure belief that we had indeed passed the turn-off was tossed around with more seriousness than imaginable. When we made the sharp right and ran down the hill toward the lights of the lodge, the two of us acted as though the journey to Mecca had been attained. We laughed, hugged one another and jumped up and down outside the bingo arena. We did not have to imagine we were women warriors of the mountain; we *were* women warriors. We had hiked eight miles all for the sake of ice cream, played the parts of the spies slinking through town, survived dead chickens, forgiven one another for each other's loss of mind and seen what the other was made of. We were survivors. Ed and Nora pulled into the lodge parking lot to pick us up five minutes after we had returned. We drove back to the cabin, the way we had come. Four miles and four minutes later, we sat on the cabin bar stools, eating ice cream and chicken, laughing at our idiocy and moralizing that food could get one into more trouble than a lake full of bats and boys.

The story does not end there. It grows in its true humor and bizarity for peculiar actions often occur in sets of twos and threes when recollecting the life and times of pre-teens. The next day we went down to the lake to go toobing with Ed and Nora. Kasey and I laid out on our towels in the sun, pretending we were not there with parents, imagining we had driven ourselves down alone, or better yet were laying on the sands of Puerto Rico instead of the sands of Skull's County. The white sand was black, the water was azure blue instead of a murky olive green and we were tribal women of the Congo, fighting off unsuitable suitors as we did tigers, with spears.

Nora swam around the docks and Ed boated off down the outlet on the left side of the Lake. I told him that there was a pretty stream with a series of bridges if he would just follow the stream along the left bank. Since I could remember, Ed had always been the jokester of all jokesters. April Fool's Day was every day for him and he had a way of setting booby traps and letting us fall into the punch line whenever he had the chance. The moment we weren't paying attention, clocks would be set back an hour, drinks would suddenly have Tabasco at the bottom and cars would begin to roll just as we were about to step foot inside, never failing to be snickered at in front of school when he had carpool. Our warrior-like success of the prior evening had Kasey and I feeling mighty cocky and we had decided before we packed up to come down to the lake that the day had come for Ed to finally receive his up and comings.

The Congo sounded, the drums beat softly and Kasey and I hauled our beach bags to the unpleasant, quite smelly and almost never used bathroom about thirty feet from the water. There, we pulled out the Noxzema, cloves, red pepper powder, and black eyeliner, all intending to make us look like jungle mercenaries with the war paint to go along with it.

Once our faces were finished and our bodies smelled like a toxification tank, we grabbed branches off of the manzanita trees at the side of the brick wall and stuck them over our swimsuits and all around our hair. When we were finished, we had only to make it over to the outlet where Ed had to be well down under the first bridge so that we could jump out in veritable jungle manner to scare the pants off him. The only problem we had not thought out was how to get down to the outlet without having all the homeowners on the beach shrieking with laughter at the sight of us. It could not be done.

Our bare feet ran through the bushes, stomping on mosquitoes, dancing to the beat of the imaginary and yet almost heard African drums. The Noxzema began to melt and the sunbathers watched the scene with wonder and fright. We jetted past the lake and through the manzanitas covering the stream of the outlet until we heard him, whistling, rowing the little boat down under the second bridge. "Ooga, Ooooga, OOOga, Ooooga, Ooga," we chanted with all might turned against our desire to laugh at one another's appearance. "Ooga, Ooooga, OOOga, Ooooga, Ooga," again we sang until Ed looked up and threw the oars into the bushes. We leaped out into the water, Kasey nearly falling into the jetty. I swerved and danced the dance of the African Oooga Queen. Kasey regained her stance and began to swim in circles about the boat, trying not to wash the conglomeration from her mug. Ed leapt from the boat and began to swim back to the lake screaming as he moved. We each dove down into the hazy waters, past the weeds clinging to the bottom of the lake before the outlet met with the larger body of water. Surfacing at the lake, feet away from Nora basking in her inner tube, we watched as Ed turned around and saw our clean faces and the tops of our heads still adorned with a sprig or too of brush popping up above the water. He began to laugh, laughing with the bellow of a jokester, the sheep that had had the wool pulled over his eyes by the Congo Oooga Queens.

And that's it. That is the way I will always see Kasey, the African Queen, the young girl devout of the ability to be embarrassed, ready to try new things, eager to live a life she loves, searching to uncover that once again, that moment of sweet natural high, laughter and that sense of the small battle being won.

When the ghosts of my guilty conscience try to haunt me, when I think of my childhood friend, the girl with my accent, my exact taste in music, my knack for dying hair, finding a bargain, the one ritualistically watching *Entertainment Tonight*, I worry that she will wind up in some sort of jeopardy, after a bad night on the town with a once seemingly kind and alluring Schizophrenic young gentleman. I fear her compassion will get the best of her and then I remember that it was me, who in the time of crisis, wanted to get into the truck, it was me who lay marred at the side of the road via dead chicken. It was Kasey who would not sleep in the ditch. It is Kasey who so boldly asks, "Can I come over to your house today?" It is *Kasey* who believes the San Antonio River is died green and I later find out she is right. It is Kasey who flies out to the place where promises were practiced and yet painfully not so fulfilled. It is Kasey, who despite her trepidation has caused me to know the value of my life and compelled me to forsake my fears. It is finally my turn to put on that purple gypsy hat; you know the one with the pearl and rhinestone quarter moon on the front to play the part of Madame Zelda.

I sit before the imaginary crystal ball and say, "Kasey, I see great things in your future." (You must read these words with a really good Greek accent in your head.) I rub my temples because the hat is really tight after all these years and say, "Kasey, your story is that of the strong journey woman. You will be remembered for your joy, ability to walk great distances, dance well to the beat of the Conga drum, speak in tongues, laugh in times of trouble, help those crazies and manage to still feel compassion for all those Candeleros. I see you dancing, child. You are sorry. I know you really did have a good time, you just realize a little later than most. I see you chanting and when you are sad and feeling lonely you will hear the voices calling, the voices that say, 'Ooga, Ooooga, OOOga, Ooooga, Ooga...'" And then I see no more.

Mel McCabe

Waiting for Tom

779-4974. That's his number. It's been at least five, six years since I've dialed it to hear a recognizable voice on the other end, but I still dial it. Thinking maybe, just maybe he'll answer. Sometimes I don't think at all. I just dial. I forget. I forget that he's gone. I forget what his voice used to sound like, but then there's that smell, that resonates in the hall of our new apartment that throws my mind thousands of miles and three floors up along that old curved wooden banister on California Street, through that beautiful old San Francisco glass door with the sheer off-white fabric pulled across the runner so tightly. That smell has me standing inside his apartment, looking through the window out onto the fire escape, past canvas, chalk, paint, half-finished works of clowns, jesters and ballerinas, always ballerinas with tutus saluting the sun and toes cramped and pointed. Jesters with sad expressions and those clowns, those clowns that always looked too much like him to let even one go after he had gone. For that was really all that was left after he had left. Those clowns. I never knew that the last time I saw him, would be the last. I suppose no one ever knows. I find it even more difficult now to visualize standing in that old apartment, but I can still see it, feel the rub of the corduroy olive green couch on my cheek and remember where it stemmed that I now find myself loving bathrooms with two doors, always searching for another one that will open up into a closet, a closet full of flannel and down. It is when I close my eyes, close them tightly in the hall of my new apartment that the smell filters up my nose warming my eyelids with memory of that light that would flood through the one window in the white-washed room where he'd paint. I hold back tears and exhale visions of the television always on and the gas always burning, the walls always changing and the paint forever being pushed out from the tiny circular openings of the oil tubes. Magenta and mint green, men with complacent faces and used young girls looking down in sadness, old Mexican women looking for their sons and soldiers slithering through the fields of the Mekong Delta. It's a horrible smell, the one in the hall, to people who have no time or memory to couple it with an emotion such as love. I heard our neighbor, Velma, loudly say, "Chao, what the hell is that rank stench coming from the stairs?"

Chao hollered back, "I think it's from the old woman downstairs who's always cooking sweet potatoes."

To think how loosely I use the term 'love' as I inhale the air out there, but for me there really was no love before him. Of course there was motherly love and fatherly love and that lusty thing that often exists between teenagers often confused for love, but not unconditional love, true non-judging adoration. That's what I felt for him. I suppose one cannot ask for such an emotion to emanate from just anyone and to find that common bond can really only rarely be sensed between two people who might not even know how much they have in common. They merely sense it. To think I never knew the man after fifteen and yet still love him more than anyone. To think there is so little left and yet…there is *something* left.

My cousin was probably the most misunderstood man in our family and saying that means a lot when considering my mother has some seventy-two living relatives. I would have to limit my statement to 'man' because my mother and I tend to find ourselves pretty misunderstood at times. When they found him in Detroit, towards the end, he had been missing for quite a few weeks and then there was that call. He was just sitting there, at the counter of the old Altman brothers' dinner downtown and my Uncle James went down and picked him up. None of us knew how the hell he got himself out there. He was half-mad, left with only half a mind of memories, and yet somehow he trekked it from San Francisco to downtown Detroit, without a car, without remembrance. I guess in the end, even though they didn't want him back home, he figured he needed to be there one last time. It's funny how often it works that way, how you find yourself wanting to go home, making a last mad dash back to the womb if only during the holidays even though your presence has not been requested. I do believe the unwanted want more than anyone, except for maybe those who are wanted wrongly.

When he died, I remember my mother coming into my room and all I could do was stare at the wallpaper in utter disbelief. How I hated that wallpaper. Blue and white tiny flowers that seemed to form faces that watched me in my sleep. I didn't allow myself to cry until she left the room. I just stared at that ugly wallpaper, the one flower face in the left corner that two years prior had taken the shape of a vicious Chinese dragon and listened to my mother talk to my father through the crack in the door.

"I think it'd be best if you stayed here with the girls and I just went back for the funeral. They have so much to do that I don't think they should miss school or we should disrupt their lives right now."

But it was too late. My life had already been disrupted. There was so much more than a tiny blemish or a minute scar on my soul. There was a gash the size of Sacramento in place of where my heart had once been. There was an echo of how he'd laugh when I'd ask him to remove his false tooth for me once again. There was the sound of his pleading to be let out, when I'd lock him in my room because I did not want him to go home. There was the understanding in his large brown saucer-like eyes, just like mine, that held the pain of what it was like to be different. There were his obscenities being shouted toward every woman who cut him off on the freeway that made me laugh and my mother sometimes roll her eyes. There was his love of cheap food, black coffee and *Barney Miller*. All this remained a film on my mind and yet it was too little to amount to much. But there were always his paintings.

My mother went to his apartment and went through the paintings. I don't remember if I went with her or not, somehow I think I did, but much of my teenage years are a blur, memories lay at the bottom of red oceans of Walker and others buried deep at the bottom of bottles cast out the windows of speeding cars. I do see myself at Ted's though. I see myself carefully placing the next canvas closer to the one leaning against my knee, thumbing through his sketches and zipping them up into leather-bound folders, wondering where our favorite had flown to and then knowing that another relative must have gotten there first. That one painting, the lone clown face, a crying clown with a diamond painted about each eye was nothing short of Ted's face looking down on me, yet expanded and so much larger than life, three by five inch eyes, a head the size of a mutant watermelon. Yet the winds of fate must have not wanted us to have it, or so my mother consoled me. We took all the rest. I claimed the one of the half-naked John Lennon, the sad man in black dreaming of circus showgirls and of course all of the Spanish palaces. Every girl needs a picture of a palace to look up at before she falls asleep.

So I dream, still today, I dream of the funeral. I was told it was raining. The pallbearers carried him through the mud and all the relatives in Michigan went and said goodbye, even those who didn't approve of him. Sometimes I kneel in the mud, in my dreams. I dig my hands into the earth and ask him to forgive me for having not said goodbye and then I secretly thank my mother for having not allowed him to shut the door on my delusions. As long as I hold off, I can believe he is still here, maybe still just missing, hitch-hiking the planet, patronizing another diner, screaming at another bad driver on a parallel freeway, laughing at a *Barney Miller* re-run, maybe in Boston or even Amsterdam. Sometimes to think that is enough, but at other times, the ones when I call and hear nothing or the voice of a young Asian girl saying, "You have called here before, please, he not live here anymore," it is a far cry from being normal, from being at peace.

There will come a time for me to move, hell it seems as though I find myself moving every five months or so in some bizarre attempt to break a Guinness Book Record. There will come a time when the smell will disappear, the touch of that corduroy couch will be found too vague to remember against my cheek and his paintings seem too large to carry along on a plane ride or in my pocket. There will come a time when I will forget just how he pulled off that tooth trick and when the obscenities I scream at all bad drivers will be remembered as my own and not stemming from the root of my favorite relative. There will come a time when all that may be left are the sounds. The music I play over and over, tapes, CD's, eight-tracks, the same ones I remember so vividly trickling out over the air of that lit room, pounding out over the pictures, painting by heavy percussion, sketching by the pain in a growled tenor. It was a voice of a overly used denizen. It was the screams of a vagabond with a tale to tell. It was the mood of many painters in anger and sadness, the voice that stuck there in the doldrums, right with them. It was the man who sung of rainbirds, raindogs, bad livers, broken hearts, pasties and g-strings, New Orleans and drinking pianos. He invited us down into the blues.

It was almost a year after Ted's death that I found myself inside a music store, holding onto a Tom Wait's *Rain Dogs* tape. Not exactly knowing what had propelled me to the section, why I was shelling out my spending money, normally designated for nothing outside of pill or bottle form, but I bought it. I didn't know at the time that it was Ted who had picked it out for me, Ted who was calling down to me, reminding me that he was watching. If you don't believe in such things, then believe it nothing more than a coincidence, but the music was Ted's voice, to me. I wore the tape out after five weeks or so and have gone through many more since then. I can't say that I know the exact appeal or just why my cousin liked Tom's music so much. I can say that for a gay man from the Midwest, it was probably not unlikely that it was soothing to hear such a voice of pain, the voice of a man who tangoed 'til he was sore, spoke of death and insanity, shame and blind love, gun street girls and prostitutes with the names of donuts. The first night I heard Tom's voice outside of Ted's place, at sixteen in my best friend's Chevrolet Nova, nursing a fifth of Smirnoff, I felt more than soothed. For the first time in a long time, since maybe lazy afternoon chalk drawing in Ted's studio. I was still wasted and wounded and yet I felt, understood.

Many would never believe that a sixty-something-year-old man and a teenager could ever hold a bond, and yet for every blank page I look at, it is nothing less than the same blank piece of paper I know Ted saw before he'd begin to paint. Paint brushes and pen, block paper and canvases, white butcher sheets and blank screens pose the same to us. For every work I finish is as good as Ted thought his work, not good enough at all. For every lady on the freeway I flip off, Ted is with me. I ride in his dusky blue-gray Tempo into sleep at night. I lock him in my room. I thank him for my visions, for my art, for the voice that gives me back my memories, for the voice that waltzes with me back into myopic visions of tenderness and innocent times where our common cynicism *was* an art, was a glorious laugh meant to cure my young loneliness that could only have been inherited and his who could only be cured by commonality or maybe even death.

Last summer, at Graceland, Vivian and I emerged from the old film room and she turned to me with a look of absolute skepticism and a complete lack of comprehension plastered upon her mug, "How the hell could those people ever feel such obsession for one human? I mean that is all the man was, a man, and yet it looks as though the way they cried and screamed, they would have sawed off their arms for Elvis!"

I smiled because I think I understood a little more, not enough to say I would have been one of the screaming and obsessed had I been born two decades earlier, but I understood. I had been raised to feel admiration for those who graced the red carpet. I had been taught to respect a man with a guitar and a song caught in his throat. I had been forced into piano lessons, guitar lessons, emerging to become what I thought was a poet, a songwriter or at least an enthusiast and I too loved Elvis. I was the daughter of a convertible Caddie driving Mama. I didn't know there were people who didn't love Elvis.

No one would ever see me throw myself full throttle into the tornado of obsession as long as I believed I would be one of them someday. I was only credits and reviews shy of becoming one of the red carpet-walking fame-filled citizens of Hollywood and TV-land. But just because I could not propel myself into putting another human being on a pedestal above myself, didn't make me any less a fan of the famed. It just made me a strong willed feminist who felt compelled to own every word Tom Waits had ever sung, including the tape with the picture of the nudie girl, back arched up against her stripper dressing room in nothing but her stilettos and silver pasties. Every song he ever wrote about, every drinking piano, every bourbon-sodden gent, every tragic gypsy, drunken lover, town with no cheer, bathtub full of gin and fifth of Old Crow strangely kept me out of trouble and flew me up on those black wings next to Ted, closer to my memories.

I love Tom, I love his voice I mean. I don't *know* the man, but he knows me. I'm the one with troubled braids. I'm the girl with the long face in the town with no cheer. I've hung my head down for sorrow. I've seen the streets turn blue and had nothing to capture a man's heart. I've tried to pace myself to make it all last and then tried to squeeze all my life into a two-day pass. It is me with the sailor's mouth and the wounded eyes. Mostly, I'm the dry local grazier and there's no refreshment for this thirsty jackaroo. He knew Ted too. He's the boy at Union Square, busting his ass 'til doomsday, never forgetting to say his prayers. He's punched a hole in the nighttime and his head is spinning round. He came home from the war with a party in his head. He lit out for California and now is doing the obituary mambo.

I love Tom. Tom is what I have left of Ted. And it proved so ironic when Derrick said to me, "So just what does this Ted Waits sing?"

I smiled, knowing he had no idea how he had slipped and in a way not slipped at all. "It's Tom Waits, Derrick, not Ted."

"Oh, I was beginning to wonder. Ya' know Ted Waits is a big wig in the computer industry and I thought you had gone techi on me or something."

The idea of me "going techi" was about as likely a thought as giving up coffee or chocolate and I smiled and rolled my eyes. When I looked in *The Chronicle* and one day earlier discovered that the *Continental Club*'s line-up had been switched around, I decided to peruse the rest of Saturday Night's options. It was *South by Southwest*, yet another year of Austin's live music festival showcasing some seven-hundred bands for the price of one admission into some fifty clubs all for the purpose of getting musicians signed and getting ticket buyers inebriated and as jovial as humanly possible. *Antone's, Atomic Café, Austin Music Hall, Babes, Back Room*, I went on down the list 'til I hit *The Paramount* and felt my heart burst out through my chest. Tom Waits. 11:30 p.m. Tom was playing *The Paramount*. The man who *never* played live, never toured, never showed his face outside a random and rare benefit was gracing Austin, TX, land of the original relaxed slacker attitude and utopic town of liberal unpretentiousness. It was too bizarre a concept to be true. I called Toni and of course Vivian and relayed the message the paper had divulged with troubled breathing and lapses of thoughts of fainting.

"So do you think that this means that anyone with a wristband will get into the venue?" I asked Viv.

Vivian's voice on the other end, sounded much like the one that came out of the Graceland theater, "Calm down. You're gonna get in. I just hope that it's not a movie about Tom Waits or some sort of misprint. I just don't think I could take living with a disappointed unmanic George. It's like Beattlemania of the nineties, isn't it?"

I too felt sorry for her. I didn't know what my nerves were capable of at that point. Hell, this was the man who had given me control of my emotions once again for nearly a decade. I did what all alkies on the wagon, five years up and a non-smoker to boot, do. I drank a pot of black coffee with half a cup of sugar 'til my hands shook like the California earth of '89. I picked Derrick up from the airport and lunged at him with my exciting news just as he stepped off the plane. It seemed to take us hours to get up to Austin. I forgot my ID when we were halfway there and the ninety-five mile an hour trip thus far took a turn ninety-five miles an hour back and then back again until it really did take us as long as it seemed to drive the seventy miles up from San Antonio. I didn't break the promise I made to myself and secretly to the others to bury my excitement of my luck in between trips to a dozen other clubs and the sounds of some twenty other bands. Time was a blink of an eye to Saturday and our hotel room was remembered as nothing more than a couple of hours slept and split between the two days that brought us to the weekend. Then there it was, as clear as it was written on the grand marquee outside of *The Paramount*: Tom Waits. We sat across the street on Congress in the plush brown velvet couch of the coffeehouse, drinking what else but the last liquid nectar of the gods, waiting for a few more friends to blow into town from Houston. Two hours later, we discovered their car had broken down and found ourselves walking over to *The Paramount* to stroke my last nerves of doubt that it might indeed be merely a Tom Waits film night. It was not, but it was *sold out*.

I don't even remember walking up to the box office, just being held up by my elbow with Vivian's hand and asking the man behind the glass with the high pitched voice, "I don't understand. I thought that if you had a wristband and were in line they'd take the first thousand or so?"

"Well, they announced it yesterday on the radio that twelve hundred of the tickets would be given out to industry people and people with badges and then only two hundred would be sold at forty bucks a pop to those in line this morning. People were camped out since four in the morning."

I turned to Viv and rolled my eyes to the back of my head with a heavy sigh, "I can't believe we were here, downtown at almost four. I would have waited in line, had I known! I could shit balls right now. I'm so pissed! What the hell are they doing just giving one-thousand two hundred tickets out to industry people when it's not like they're gonna sign him to a new contract and half those people probably don't even give a shit about going!"

Vivian looked at me and shook my shoulders in a desperate motion so as not to have me go into unnecessary angered and desperate hysterics. "George, just listen to yourself. You've got some six hundred people out there, like you said with badges that don't give a shit whether they get in tonight or not, so you just have to buy a ticket off one of them. I'm not gonna go home with you having not seen Tom. Don't worry."

I turned back toward Derrick, spent on disappointment and looked backward at Viv to see her already talking with one of Waits' men from the show. Quickly walking over to join them, I hoped to aid her in her current pursuit of syrupy sweet-talk poured thickly with the intent upon him lapping it up long enough to sneak us into the bathroom where I might hide until Tom's voice could seduce me out of the stall.

"Where you girls from?"

"San Francisco," I found myself blurting out as I was shot a disapproving glance from Vivian that told me I should not have offered the information of originating from such a metropolitan mecca. I had only figured that if we mentioned a place further than Austin, he might feel sorry enough for us, thinking we had hiked it some two-thousand miles from home and slip us two tickets. Both of our imaginations had run rampant, as our efforts were soon lost on the earless and compassionless roadie.

"San Francisco! Perfect! Tom's thinking of doing a concert there, so you see if you just wait awhile, you can see him right at home."

"Well we don't exactly live there anymore. We live in Texas now, San Antonio, so we'd have to fly back there to see him and who knows if he'll really play there or how many tickets will be available then and he's here right now."

"You're not listening to me. I just told you that he'll probably be in Frisco soon and better yet, you don't live there, cause you can take a trip back home and see all your old pals and familia and see Mr. Waits too."

I smiled a half smile and turned around before rolling my eyes. We had gotten nowhere. The thought of having to go back to San Francisco to only *maybe* see Tom when he was right there in Austin, probably laying atop his bed at *The Driskill* down the street if I imagined him right, was depleting my energy of all positivity.

I looked at Viv and quickly saw how much of a stake she had in getting me in as I did. I was not an easy person to live with as an unhappy and downtrodden melodramatic, it was hard enough living with the melodrama alone. I allowed Derrick and Viv to stand on either side of me as they each cajoled promise back into my veins that it was indeed gonna be all right. I began to do the math as to how much money I could really afford to take out of the bank to pay the scalpers. I couldn't afford any, but I took our three hundred and we stopped by the bookstore to look up the moderately legalized yellow page scalpers. The lady at the bookstore let us use the phone until her boss walked by for the fourth time, twenty two numbers later, and asked us how much we were willing to pay for our next phone call. We tromped off to the only place that said they still had tickets, but by the time we got there they were gone. He was selling them for five-hundred apiece anyway and the lady there told us that we were better off just going down to *The Paramount* a few hours before the show and scoping the situation out for ourselves.

I resigned myself to the free concert at the park and gorged my hungry heart on a bag of Bird Eggs, not to be confused with jellybeans for they really are far superior in taste, although they do not contain the black ones that would round off perfection. Our friend from Houston and her foreign friends thought me more than an odd American girl with my shaking hands and incessant nervous chatter. I laid down on the lawn and allowed myself to be photographed for prosperity by Vivian who undoubtedly thought the moment of stress and anxiety just another incident of common hysterics in the chronicles of Melodramatic George. To pacify the rapid heartbeats of my heart and the justifiable stomach hunger of our friends, we headed off to Sixth Street to try and find a less crowded spot to eat before the fest crowd extended the wait to an hour. I played the part of the horrible conversationalist during dinner and hardly directed a single question to our new friends or our old one. I managed to suck down a little lettuce and a cup of coffee before Viv and Derrick and I all abandoned the others to go and stand out in front of the theater to begin the bargaining. The two of them made their loud pleas for me not to just hand over all of my money to the first bidder before we arrived.

"Will you guys just promise me, you'll go and leave me alone when we get there? I want you two to go and have a good time. Go to Liberty Lunch or *Antone's*. Don't waste your last night trying to get me in to see him."

They both rolled their eyes as if I had told them to drop me off at the gates of St. Peter with nothing but the wiles of an attorney and a used car salesman. As it turned, out I could have used some of those 'used car salesman techniques' because I soon found myself at the piranha tank. We were literally the *only* women on the sidewalk of more than fifty and Viv, the eternal woman dead set against ever using feminine wiles to get anything, told me to take off my sweatshirt and extend the pout in my mouth. We walked up to a scraggly looking ex-surfer, long blond hair, beard, pop belly, a professional scalper. "I'm not selling my ticket until I get another. If you want one after I get another then I'll sell it to ya for one and a quarter, but I'm working for the big timers and they need two good seats."

I looked at Viv and knew that she had gotten about as much out of that explanation as I had. If the guy needed two tickets then why was he gonna sell me one when he had the other? Why not just sell me the one right now, for hell, one and fifty and then we could be on our way before nine o'clock, see two bands and I could waltz on up at eleven twenty six?

I thought that was a pretty decent argument but the surfer would have none of it, "Look, I told you. I am not selling my ticket! NO deal! No deal girlie! Just back off. I need another ticket." He had a large yellow sign that read, "Buying tickets." Five other guys approached him and got the same scowled reproach, with more finesse than mine. I spotted a twenty-five-year-old guy standing in the archway of the theater, sucking on this tongue stud with a half-wretched grin spread across his thin lips. I walked up to him and asked if he was selling.

"Yeah, but I'm selling two. Ya need two?"

"No just one, but why don't you just sell me the one and you're not gonna have any trouble selling the other. Nobody thinks they're gonna get to sit together tonight anyway or gives a shit if they do."

"Yeah, nobody *thinks* they're gonna, but that's the beauty of these two puppies. I can sell these for a primo price because they *are* together."

"How much you sellin' 'em for?"

"Three-hundred apiece."

"You're fuckin' high! Where the hell you from?"

"Vancouver."

I smiled and put my hand on my hip, "People from Austin are never gonna pay three apiece for those."

"How you figure? You're out here and not everyone is from Austin."

"Yeah, well they're not from Canada either, you're fuckin' high."

"These two tickets are gonna pay for my badge."

"Your badge didn't cost ya six-hundred. You're such a liar."

"Nah, it did and my airfare down here! These are primo seats too. I heard that every seat in this place is good, but these are the last two rows in the balcony and supposedly the acoustics are the best at the back since they bounce from the stage first right up to the top."

"You are such a used car salesmen. I've been in this theater half a dozen times and who the hell ever heard of the last seats being the best? What a scammer. Look, I'll give you two hundred for one and you'll be able to get two, maybe one fifty for the other and that's the most you're gonna get the whole fuckin' night. I guarantee it." I felt Viv's eyes burn into the side of my right cheek, as she grew angered at the fact that my initial offer was so high, but I just wanted the hell off the drag. It was nine and I figured that fifty bucks higher than Viv would have started at was worth the fact that I could get her and Derrick out of here and down to the Lunch where they could stop feeling sorry for me and cease wasting their evening. The guy wouldn't budge.

"No fuckin' way. You know it and I know it. I'm getting six hundred easy for these two."

I looked over at the husky Armenian guy pacing the street about ten feet away from us and walked up to him. "Are you trying to buy?"

"Ya, but I'm not willing to go two hundred. I'll go one and fifty tops, but not two hundred. That's insane." He looked shifty but desperate. The aging surfer looked over at me and shouted, "I'm not selling. I told you I'm not selling!"

Viv rolled her eyes and scowled back, "We know! We know!"

Derrick had already walked over to the other side of the theater and was working on a guy who had been one of the four in the morning crowd to show up to buy one of the two hundred released tickets to the non-industry people. I was beginning to feel horrible that he and Viv wouldn't just leave and go and have a good time.

"Would you two just go and get out of here. Look at Derrick. He is having a miserable time and you, you know I'm gonna get a ticket if I have to sell my soul."

"That's what I'm afraid of. I don't wanna see you get screwed. Do you realize that you are the only chick in front of this place?"

I looked around and saw some fifteen, twenty men all brewing about the place. Two mode college boys sat on the curb with looks of shear frustration as we already knew they weren't going over sixty bucks apiece. We had a crew of Euro-boys all willing to shell out one hundred apiece getting turned down. There was a deadhead group all in line at the ticket window in hopes that the ticket lady would take a twenty-fifth look at their pathetic faces and just spontaneously, with absolutely no authority, begin issuing newly printed tickets for the zero seats that remained in the theater. I walked back over to the Canadian sleazoid and told him that the Armenian and me were willingly to go three fifty for the both of 'em.

"You wanna sit next to *that* guy? No way. I'm not gonna sell the other ticket to that guy. He wouldn't even go two hundred anyway. If you can find another dude to go two hundred than maybe, but not him."

"You know you're not gonna sell it to me for two, you're just waiting to see if you can get six for the both of 'em."

Viv looked up at the guy and retorted, "We're only paying one fifty anyway."

He looked down at Viv and smiled. "Why the hell don't you wanna go? I'll sell the two to the both of you for four."

"She doesn't wanna go," I shot back, "I mean she wants to, but for her wristband and that's it. She just wants to see me get a ticket, not get screwed and then be on her merry way. Anyway, just fuck it. I'll buy a ticket off one of these kids who's gonna show up with a badge and not even know who the hell Tom Waits is. He'll unload it for seventy-five and you'll be the one with the frown on your puss."

The sleaze smiled and gave a little laugh, "You're good. You're real good." He grabbed my stomach and pinched it, "Don't think I didn't see that hip swagger and that little show of the stomach to keep me pacified, nope though, I'm getting three for each of these." Viv leaned over after having seen the stomach pinch and glared at the guy as she pulled a mock lesbian number by pulling off imaginary fuzz balls from my sweater.

The guy was high. I was getting irritated and walked five feet closer to the curb, further from the archway, from the Canadian ball-buster. Viv and I peered down at Derrick who looked as though he were about to fall asleep. I shivered as my sweatshirt and sweater hung over the loop in my backpack strap. I sucked in, pushed out and looked down the front of the theater past the red carpet in hopes of widening my scope of scalpers. The same archway hanging, tongue-pierced, sleazy resident of Vancouver sauntered back up the sidewalk toward us two. "So what's this Tom Waits like? I don't get all the hype. I've never even heard the guy."

Shist! This was the exact crap that really had the ability to piss the shit out of me. It was no big deal that Derrick thought Tom was Ted Waits or that Viv thought he was only moderately more gifted than Garth Brooks, but to hear from a ball-busting scalper who would go down no less than three hundred, that he did not even know what the hell he was selling was just too much. "You know what? How the hell do you even know how much those tickets are worth if you don't even know your commodity?" I asked him with a sly grin as I leaned into his face with a subtle eyelash flutter.

"Hell, I've heard the hype. I gotta friend here who waited in line for a front row and was offered five for his."

"Yeah, well that's front row. I don't even give a shit where I'm at, but I'm not paying three for the last row, I'm not paying three for the fuckin' front."

"So what the hell does this guy sing."

"Nothing you'd ever hear off the radio, not in Texas anyway, hell not on the coast either. You've probably heard his covers. Springsteen sang his '*Jersey Girl*,' Rod did '*Downtown Train*' and The Eagles covered '*Ol' 55*.' I guess you mighta seen the movie '*Dead Man Walking*.' He did the soundtrack for that. He's done a few soundtracks actually, award winning ones, and a dozen or so movies too-"

"Oh yeah, '*Dead Man Walking*' with Johnny Dep, good flick."

I looked over at Viv and affirmed with one side grin that we were indeed dealing with a moron if Sean Penn was being mistaken for Johnny. I backed away from the Canadian upon Viv's initiation and closer to the lesser of two evils, the aging surfer as Elijah Wood walked out the front door of *The Paramount* and into a Lincoln town car where his parents already sat in the back.

"Isn't that that kid from that movie?" Viv asked.

"Yeah, he's from that movie *The Man Without a Face* and *The Good Son* and hell I can't remember the whole slew of others."

"God, that kid's short."

"Hell, they all are. Remember Tom Cruise? He's like what? Five-six, and Eddie Vedder's like five-three or something? You don't have to be tall on a screen or on a stage."

"That's true."

"Will you two just get out of here? Look at Derrick. He looks pathetic. This is no way to spend your last night up here. It's like you said," I looked down at my watch, "It's only ten and I'll bet a whole shitload of people aren't gonna line up 'til like eleven and I'm just gonna have to deal with my panic attacks and take a chill 'til the less agro ticket holders arrive. I'll get a ticket. Just go."

"I know you will, but I just hate this male saturated sleaze haven. I feel like I'm leaving you at the gates of hell."

"Oh please, it's such a perfect story. I'll be fine, really, go." I had grown so cold that I knew that I had few arguments left within and one more refusal to leave and I would find myself nothing more than happy to have them there if only to keep my mind off the growing cold. I bit my lip, shivered and turned to see Derrick walking past the red carpet with a smile on his face. He was holding a ticket and Viv jumped and ran toward him.

It took me more than a second to realize what had happened and even then it did not fully register until Derrick had secretly emerged with the ticket from his pocket, "One Ted Waits ticket" he said as he motioned for me to immediately put it in hiding.

I laughed and jumping up into the air again and do not even recall coming down. It really was a Ted Waits ticket, entrance into the sounds of the voice of Tom to regain the feeling of being with Ted. I was home. I was ecstatic. I had paid one and a quarter for a ticket that started at five when I had been willing to go to three.

I turned toward the Canadian sleaze, jumped over the carpet and flashed my ticket in his face, seat U5, three rows closer than his two, like I gave a shit if I were seated on the ceiling, strapped to the center chandelier hanging upside down. "One twenty-five!"

Vancouver smiled a genuine smile this time, "I'm happy for ya, have a good time. Maybe I'll see ya inside."

We crossed Congress and cut over to Lavaca heading down to *Antone's* with free hearts and no anxiety. Nothing was gonna kill this high, little could compare to the natural euphoria I felt at that moment. "How the hell did you get the guy down to one and a quarter?!"

"Well I knew you'd kill me if I the guy laughed at my offer, but he was gonna give it to me for one fifty. I told him no way, it was one twenty-five or no deal and he hesitated before saying okay."

"I would have shot you if he walked away at that offer."

"Oh tell me about it. I risked, I totally risked, but hell, I thought if I walked back with the ticket for one twenty-five you'd die. And Viv and I were talking earlier that we couldn't believe you were gonna pay two or three, that was just insane. I hated that Canadian jerk and was just dying to out buy him by a load."

"I woulda paid two, if it just meant getting out of there before the line started and before I bust an aneurysm."

"I know you woulda, but I just had to try for one twenty-five."

"You are *so* fuckin' rad Derrick! Thank you, thank you, thank you soooo much. This means so much to me! You have one happy Georgia on your hands!"

He laughed. Viv laughed. We all laughed our asses off all the way down to *Antone's* as I exclaimed, "I couldn't be happier on my wedding day."

I waited in line outside *Antone's* to see *The Scars* with Viv and Derrick until about twenty after eleven and then went running up Lavaca to Fifth, turning up Congress where I saw a sight to astound. There was a line wrapped around *The Paramount* and down a good six blocks of some five to six thousand people all with the delusion they were getting into the theater to see Tom. I began to walk to the end of the line and after a good two minutes and three blocks later began to ask people, "Do you guys all have tickets?" They all exclaimed and affirmed that they indeed did, but I was beginning to figure out that these people believed that just because they had badges and wristbands they thought they were gonna prance on in. Now don't get me wrong, I felt bad, really bad, I do not mean to make light of their plight, but I was not one of them. I had been one of the ticketless an hour prior, but I was not intending on waiting in line with the ticketless when I had exactly six minutes to get into that theater and up into my moonbeam, howl a cry at the stage and not be heard seat. I turned around at the end of the third block and began to walk back up to the theater. When I had reached the front of the line I saw my old husky Armenian buddy and casually sauntered over to him as

I received glaring looks from the men behind him. "How much you end up paying?" I asked.

He smiled a smile I had not received even a dose of before when intentions had been serious and in competition with my own finagling, "One fifty. There was no way I was gonna pay two."

"Good for you."

"How 'bout you?"

"One twenty-five."

"You're kidding!"

"No, my friend from LA bargained a badger down."

"Damn, that'd great. That's where I'm from, LA."

"I'm sorry. At least you're here now."

"Yeah, well, I moved here about eight years ago, but I miss it a lot. I wanna go back."

"You're kidding? Whadda you miss more, the smog, the traffic, the cell phones plastered to drivers' ears or is it the quaint feeling of the town?"

"You miss it too?"

"No way, I'm from San Francisco, that I miss, but the prices are too gouging to ever make me really wanna go back, call it home again. Austin is the only place I could ever live now, in America."

"I hear ya, but just wait seven, eight years, you'll be singin' a different tune. You can't abolish the fast and frenzied Californian from the honorary Texan and hell you haven't lost your swindling techniques of the lawyer-like cell-phoned Californian yet. You wanna cut in?"

I smiled up at him and scooted in front just as they began to put people in single file. "You've become more of a Texan then you think. LA guys don't let people just cut in."

We laughed and began to walk to the front of the theater where I spotted the sleazy Canadian holding out his tickets, still banking on three apiece. I didn't regret not waiting. My heart would not have been able to tolerate the not knowing. I was just glad I didn't have to buy the tickets from the guy as I waved and disappeared through the glass doors. I breathed my first true sigh of relief as I walked up the stairs, into the theater and sat down into my seat. There was always that paranoid thought in the back of my mind that Derrick might have purchased a good counterfeit. But as my ass hugged onto the red velvet, I allowed my nerves to bled into my muscles and loosed my shoes as the usher seated the man next to me.

"Peanut gallery, huh?" the man next to me suggested with a shrug.

I smiled and looked down at the stage in amazement that I had made it. I was there. The wait was in fact almost over and I was trying to savor the feeling of knowing I was about to hear the voice of the man who had symbolized unconditional love and understanding to me for almost ten years. "I got my ticket pretty late so I'm just so thankful to be here."

"Really? Why'd you get it so late?"

"I had to buy from a scalper outside, since they only sold two hundred tickets outside of the industry's given ones."

"Really? My God, I had no idea." He leaned over to me and whispered, "I gotta admit to you, I've never heard any of the guy's songs before, but they gave one ticket to my band and the other six weren't interested so I decided to take a chance."

I smiled over at him and said, "There's no chance here. This is the safest bet of the festival, I could melodramatically say, in your life as well, but I'm partial. The guy's a legend though, I'll tell you that, this man is the king of all songwriters."

"Oh wow, I'm really excited, this is gonna be great. I'm Joseph."

Ted's middle name I thought as I shook Joseph's hand, "George, I'm George. Nice to meet you Joseph."

"So, do you live in Austin?"

"San Antonio, right now, but I used to live here. I'm moving back in July. Where you from?"

"Upstate New York, small town called Alfred."

"Get out!"

"You've heard of it?"

"I was there just a few weeks ago. My sister, lives there, goes to Alfred University."

"That's crazy, I teach at State, just across the street."

"Wow, what a small world. Whadda ya teach?"

"Sixties history, the whole hippie free love era, probably a little old for you, even a little old for me, but I was kinda the younger brother of someone who went through it all. By the time I was old enough go anywhere, hang out down in the Haight and enter Winterland they had just closed it down, fate huh? You probably have no idea what I'm talkin' about."

"Are you kidding me? I know exactly what you mean. If I had a time machine and could go anywhere, thoughts would bleed back to the times of Shakespeare and of course the Village in the fifties. But more than any other wish, I wanted to stand in Winterland and just listen to *The Dead* play while someone braided roses into my hair as I sat, smokin' on a peace pipe. The stories my cousin used to tell of San Francisco in the late sixties, God that's when you moved out there for better reasons then the sunshine and a good job, it was about being in a mecca that reeked of the closest breathing land to a liberal utopia. Now there's nothing left but thousand dollar studios and a job at Taco Bell *after* you get your degree."

Joseph looked at me as though I had gone mad due to the uncanny assimilation of my mind and his, "How the hell does a girl from Austin, Texas know so much about the Bay Area?"

"Hey I never said I was *from* Austin, hell nobody's from Austin, you're just lucky if you can find this place and get out here fast as you can. I was born and raised in San Francisco."

"Get outta here. Me too! That is so crazy, where exactly?"

"On the Peninsula actually."

"Me too, this is just getting more strange by the moment."

"You still got family back there?"

"Yeah, my brother and my parents. They used to live in Half Moon Bay. They're out by the Santa Cruz area now."

"That's where my parents are retiring now. Hell for what you bought your house for back in the fifties and sixties you can sell and live off that."

"Tell me about it, but I just still feel like if I would have stayed there, I would have been trapped, you know? I just wanted to see a different part of the country, make my own way. Well, you probably know you're down *here* right? I'll tell you, you picked a better climate than New York. This is gorgeous. You cannot imagine what it's like in upstate New York."

"No, I can. I didn't make it out to Texas right off the bat. I headed for Chicago first and lasted a very snowy blizzardy year before I realized that I would rather live where it doesn't snow in May."

"Oh, I hear ya, how funny." The lights began to flicker and I leaned forward with my elbows on my knees and clasped my hands in prayer. "It was so nice to meet you George. Look if you're ever in New York again, look me up, here's the name of my band." He pulled out a *Mectaplin* sticker and handed it to me, "I have a feeling I might see you again."

I smiled and thought he might be right as I also concluded how much he reminded me of Ted and how much he reminded me of home. The theater went dark and a blue-light shot out onto the stage, illuminating all the percussion instruments already gathered in a large circle, surrounding the slightly elevated piano. The theater went black again and then a light crept back into the curtain and emerged with Tom. Seventy-five percent of the audience began to clap politely and the other twenty-five including myself stood up and screamed. The girl next to me switched seats with her boyfriend who was undoubtedly a screamer and she resigned to clapping in her chair. From the moment he began to sing I only prayed he would never stop. He opened with *Heartattack and Vine*. He sang his old stuff, some of his new stuff, from Elektra and from the Island years. His piano was drinking. He invited us into the blues, underground, through Frank's wild years, on a downtown train, while drinking a jockey full of bourbon and we were left to clap hands. Clap hands and holler, screech the vocals of our gratitude for this man whose own voice appears to have been ripped by razors, burned in the night. Most of us never wanted that Saturday night to end. I became pseudo-girlfriend to the guy who sat to the right of me. Every time I jumped up to applaud and yell, I became the girl he wanted to be sitting to the right of him, slumped in her chair, mildly affected. Because you really either love him or you hate him. He either grabs you at the throat or doesn't manage to grab you at all, a concept morosely difficult for me to accept, but alas I remained one of possibly fifty women in the audience of fourteen hundred. I knew not many women panted for the crooner of dark melodies, our lyricist of pain. I also knew that among the thousand who had come with little recollection as to just what Tom Waits was famous for singing, probably nine-hundred were headed off to Waterloo after the show to pick up as many of his cd's as they could indeed afford. With a four hundred dollar badge slung around each neck, it looked as though the record store might pay its mortgage.

As I began to cry at the intro to *Swordfishtrombones*, I sensed Joseph crying too. My new boyfriend to the right of me had already started his salt flow at the sound of the second song. We weren't like Elvis fans, and it wasn't a nineties version of Beattlemania, but it was as close as it got for all of us. There was a feeling that night that we were sharing air with a presence in which we might never find ourselves again. The man was a showman. I only once took my eyes of the stage to gaze about *The Paramount*, resting them but for a moment at the top of the ceiling where angels are painted and I said to myself that I was indeed glad they had not held the show at the Music Hall. It's easy to say such a thing being one of the lucky ones sitting inside while others were rioting and yelling at cops holding them back out on the red carpet. Despite the fact that the Music Hall would have allowed another fifteen hundred inside, when a man only comes out once in a blue moon, the man does it right. He doesn't need the money, added fame or have a goddamn thing to prove and so he decides upon the intimate class and beauty of *The Paramount*. Hell the man hadn't been to Austin in twenty years. Just as I imagined, he admitted to staying at *The Driskill*, another touch of old class, somehow the Omni and the Music Hall wouldn't have framed him in quite the way the angels did that night. I didn't want to look up at him from the Music Hall, only to catch a standing glimpse as I jumped over tall men in black in front me. I wanted to stare down from seat U5, as each string on the bass pulled a light down, red then blue and the piano caused the whole panel to light up. I wanted to let my tears spill down toward the stage. I imagined Tom inside my very own crystal ball, just as the one I have back home and keep on my bedstand with the city inside that plays *I left my heart in San Francisco* and if I look with blurred eyes allows me to see Ted's place up on California Street in between the old toy Victorians. I wanted to hold him in the small hallowed opening of my clasped praying hands to imagine if I turned him and his piano carefully over, glitter would slowly flow down from the eyes of the angels on the ceiling and I could bring him home, turn the bottom of the stage and hear *Time* each night before I drifted off to sleep. That evening I knew I would hear it. My ears would hang onto Tom's '*Time*' and Ted would ride into my mind on the angels' wings of *The Paramount*. He'd cut off a poor flying angel, swearing and cursing like none other in his dusty blue-gray Tempo. I'd lock him in my room and not let him out until I woke. I would wake to feel the hotel pillow with the nasty lipstick stain that had been there since we had arrived three days earlier, but this time it would feel like corduroy, green couch corduroy. I'd remember the innocent dreams of Mexican women and the Vietcong dancing to *Raindogs*. They'd sway and swivel attracting the ballerinas and the jesters and the clowns, always those sad clowns who might be resigned to smile to that voice of gargling glass for just one night.

I hardly remember walking back down to Ruta Maya to meet up with Derrick and Viv. I don't even remember walking out of the theater, only hugging Joseph and my pseudo-boyfriend as they exclaimed it the best concert of their lives, beating me to the grave by at least a decade, which meant a lot. I think I floated down Congress, losing my city bitch mask usually strapped so tightly about my ears when I prepared to walk anywhere alone at night, at two thirty in the morning. Two trips around the coffee shop without finding Derrick and Vivian and I flew back up Lavaca to *Antone's,* where I spotted them through the open door, listening to *The Scars* last set. Derrick's head protruding out of his six-foot frame was not hard to discover among a room full of rather height-impaired

Texans. *The Scars* sang another song about sex and spiders and I fell back into my memories of the night and that time my sister and I took off for New Orleans. I had been listening to *Tango 'til Their Sore* and that line stuck hard in my head, "*Make sure they play my theme song, I guess daisies will have to do, Just get me to New Orleans, And paint shadows on the pews...*" And we were off. I woke the next morning, worked 'til noon and let out of Austin by one with four hundred miles trailing in the dust of our tailpipe. Tom serenaded us through every inch of the bayou, past the casinos of Saint Charles, past the prayerful stained-glass steeple of Baton Rouge until we arrived at the mouth of the Delta. We spoke with ghosts that weekend. Toni still talks about having breakfast with Ted at that open-window café on Rue Royale and I can say that I've seen him since the bayous and the Mississippi River. I think he carried me down Lavaca that Saturday night, pushed me into *Antone's* and forced his way into a corner of my head forever.

"What are you gonna do when Tom dies George?" Derrick asked me after we had all piled into Viv's tiny car and were buzzing up the Loop toward Kerbey Lane.

I thought hard upon a concept I had not wanted to entertain and then realized, "He'll never die for me. I don't think he'll ever die." The truth was, that if Ted hadn't died, how could Tom? Maybe the day I'd say goodbye to Tom, would be the day I'd stop calling Ted, but until then I'd hold onto 779-4974, wooden banisters, that smell in my hall, *Barney Miller* and ballerinas, sunshine in studios, double-door bathrooms, jesters and the Vietcong. Until then, "*It's such a sad*

Mel McCabe

old feeling. The fields are soft and green. It's memories that I'm stealing, but you're innocent when you dream...Oh, you're innocent when you dream..."

Bob Dylan, Jack Kerouac & the Rodeo

There was a sense of unabashed freedom I felt when I entered the rodeo. Whether or not that's just a bizarre paralleled association dating back to my first viewing of Clint Eastwood's *Bronco Billy's Wild West* or simply the obvious similarities the 'Big Top Cattle Show' has with a good old-fashioned carnival, I may never know. I *am* aware though that freedom, that true sense of magnanimous liberation is not achieved as easily as a crime is committed these days. I've also never seen anyone having a bad time at the carnival. I only wish I could say the same about the rodeo.

Toni and Kasey and I sat out on the bench and I watched the Ferris wheel spin colors in the night. Toni gave me a compassionate smile and looked back at

Kasey. "Well," she said, "I'm not really nuts about Earl Gray anyway."

I tried to stuff my laughter as I spit out, "I think its Collin Raye."

"I think both of you are wrong," Kasey retorted, "But I can't stand any of 'em anyway, country singers that is."

"You can't say that about *all* country music," I found myself saying with surprise, in a way that I only could find myself so altered after having lived with a country music fanatic for the past six months.

"Yes I can!" Kasey exclaimed with enough fervor to fight off a tight Wranglered attacker, big belt buckle and all.

"Well I can't really stand all these new country singers coming out the woodworks who are starting to sound a whole helova lot more like rock-a-billy than country anyway, but the old shit is still good, Johnny and Merle and everyone loves Dolly."

"Oh yeah, you gotta love Dolly!" Toni retorted with a face that was trying its hardest to hold back a tone-deaf rendition of *9 to 5*.

"I just can't stand it here!" Kasey let out with much more loudness than I had anticipated, as well as the lovebirds taking up the bench across the walkway next to the cotton candy and caramel apple truck.

Toni and I looked back at one another again before she asked, "Well Kasey, you said you wanted to come and that you were gonna try and have fun, come to think of it. It's really not that bad, what's the problem?"

I jogged my memory back to the phone call I had made earlier that day from work where Vivian had told me that she told Kasey that she was gonna go to the rodeo with Maggie and let the three of us go off and listen to some music downtown.

"Oh Viv," I had said from my cubicle at the loan office, "Are you sure? I mean I feel bad that you gotta go to the rodeo without us. We can go. I kinda wanna see what its all about anyway."

"Well, I don't want anyone going who isn't gonna have a fun time. My priority is not to drag anyone anywhere without their consent, but the weird thing is that Kasey said she really wants to go," Vivian said with some surprise in her voice.

"She did?"

"Yeah," Viv responded, "I know you said she has had some bad rodeo experiences, but when I told her the plan, she said that she wanted me to get tickets for all of us and that she reallly wanted to do it too, since she was visiting Texas and all. So I guess I'll order the tickets."

I thought about what I had heard as I sipped my highly doctored sugar coffee and hoped that Kasey knew what she was talking about. I mean hell, I was up for the new experience. I wanted to go to the rodeo in fact, but Kasey was the poster girl for animal rights, had no tolerance for the honky-tonk and for the life of me I could not figure out what she was gonna do when the hog-tying and calf-roping events began.

I quickly deciphered all that would be, when the five of us filed into the big top, walked up to our spots on the bleachers and Kasey began to make disgusted facial expressions in my direction. All could not be ignored by the disappointed gestures on her mug. Retching noises followed and ended with comments loud enough for Vivian and Maggie (our resident rodeo woman from work and third generation '4-H'er) to hear. Just as Viv and Toni and I were attempting to educate ourselves on the traditions of the rodeo with Maggie's detailed explanation of why the kids were trying to rope the calves, Kasey let out with, "This is absolutely disgusting," with her hand melodramatically thrown over her eyes, "I am sickened, I don't even think I can watch this, this..."

One glance in Maggie and Viv's direction told me that I outta get her the hell out of the tent before she truly offended a rancher. Past the indoor rodeo fair, I looked up at the stands and sorrowfully glanced back at Viv and Toni. Walking past the tables of homemade fudge, belt buckles, dreamcatchers and cowboy hats, I wished that we had just gone down to a club rather than come to the rodeo to play the parts of liberals in misery.

"I know you're embarrassed and pissed," Kasey said to me as we walked outside and crossed on over to the carnival.

"Let's just walk," I retorted. I knew I could not be angered with a little cotton candy in my belly and a trip through the House of Mirrors. What one thinks she knows though is not always true and the House of Mirrors most often does not distort the truth enough as it should. I *was* a little ticked.

"I'm not gonna compromise who I am, just to comply with some hicks at a rodeo," Kasey said in her defense, even though I had not mentioned anything. She did have a way of knowing I was annoyed even when I thought I had done my best at masking it.

"It's not that I was asking you to pretend you weren't an animal activist Kasey. I'm not thrilled about animal cruelty either, but I just figure that I can't get upset until I have all the info. I was trying to hear everything that Maggie was talking about. I thought that the cattle roping looked a little odd too but then…"

"It was sick! Sick and disgusting. I mean look how young they start 'em. Those kids think its all right to just run out there and have a fricken contest to see who can jump the calf first so they can go home and have a little veal for din-din."

"Kasey, no, that's just it, yeah, it was a contest, but to see who could rope their calf the fastest and then all those kids get to take the one that they chose home. Then they bring it back to the farm to raise it and see what its like taking care of the animal. I mean for all we know this kind of responsibility can lead to a lower pregnancy rate."

"It's just unbelievable. It doesn't matter, so they bring their raised cow back the next year to sell it for burgers," Kasey said with ninety degrees of cynicism.

She hadn't heard anything I had said. I agreed that my kids were probably not gonna be cow herders, nor members of 4H. On the other hand, the little that I knew about the organization was only now due mostly to the fact that I was spending my rodeo dollars on the carnival outside of the tent. I couldn't help but admit that I really did wanna see the buckin bronco bit too, even if it did involve cruelty. I loved *Urban Cowboy*, *Rhinestone Cowboy* and even *8 and a half seconds* and wanted to see the cowboys! I grew up on *Bonanza* and *Big Valley* reruns, had my first crush on Adam

Cartwright and my second on Nick Barclay, yet I consigned to the fact that we were not making it back under the tent in any kind of hurry.

I bought a slab of fudge from the vender and drowned my annoyance in chocolate. Kasey's face still showed evidence of anger at what she only perceived was going on inside. Toni came out of the tent and I scooted over onto the other side of the bench with 'the sulker.'

"You guys ever think it'd be cool to travel round with the carnival?" I asked Toni more than Kasey.

"Yeah, I think it'd be fun," Toni answered back, "You could eat all the candy covered apples you'd ever want, ride all the rides and meet a ton of people."

"A ton a hicks and weirdos," Kasey retorted.

I smiled over at her, "I dunno. I don't think people are any the stranger here than they are like in Santa Cruz. Member when we were kids and we used to love to go down to the boardwalk and gorge on salt water taffy and flirt with all the beach bums and ride the old wooden roller coaster 'til we'd get sick."

"That was different, we were just kids and hell, who doesn't appreciate a real wooden roller coaster? Plus you've got the beach down there, the beach makes it all a little less trashy," Kasey explained.

"I think the boardwalk has its own element of 'down-home,' just like the traveling carnival, but that's kinda what makes it so romantic."

"Romantic?" Kasey looked perplexed.

"I know exactly what you mean," nodded Tom.

"Yeah, it's like the last bastion of freedom. The boardwalk, the carnival, especially the carnival reminds me of Bob Dylan and Jack Kerouac."

"Bob Dylan and Jack Kerouac?"

"Yeah, its been around for awhile. The carnival is like the last safe hitchhike this country has to offer. It's a little Vegas, a little predictable, a little spark a life in an otherwise dreary town, if even just for a coupla days. The carnival's here! The rides, the candy, the lights and the games, prizes and noises, music and the House of Mirrors. The Haunted House and the unkempt men working the booths, who you just know have some good stories to tell. Boyfriends and husbands trying to impress their girls, teenagers excited to meet and check each other out somewhere off track from the regular 'A and Dub' or DQ. Throw in a rodeo to boot and you've practically got a circus. And everyone knows that a circus is only steps away from a good ol' Renaissance Fair."

Toni smiled in agreement as Kasey shook her hand in disbelief, "No way. There is no way you're gonna compare a Renaissance Fair to a circus."

"Yeah, even a carnival Kasey!" I laughed, "Let's face it, all the ambient factors are there: all the discards and crazies, the eccentrics and whimsical fools. Are the fat lady and the strong man all that different from the fifteen-year-old, dressed up in tights spouting sonnets? A carnival is essentially an exact translation of 'merry-making.' Who would disagree that the greatest rebel-rouser of celebration and games was Shakespeare's Puck? I think no one. I think that's why I love it all."

"And just how the hell are these people any more Kerouacian and Dylanesk?" Kasey asked with air of grand skepticism.

"I dunno, its just this feeling I have, this exalted sense of acceptance at the circus, at the carnival, hell, even at the rodeo. It's wild. It's untamed and anything can happen. You can win, you can lose, you have fun, fly, go round and round, get a sugar high, recognize that you're surrounded by people from all over the country. The carnival, the rodeo, the traveling ones are like buses, old buses from the fifties and sixties pickin' up the misfits, and from one misfit to a few others, I kinda feel like everyone belongs here."

"I guess I see what you're saying," Kasey said with a little more enthusiasm, hopefully enough to soon re-enter the big tent. "Did you guys go the carnival when you were kids?"

Toni walked back from the vending truck with a blue billowing cotton candy in her left hand as her right one picked away the pieces from the top, "We used to go all the time back in Michigan, when we'd get a chance to go and visit the familia for the summer, Fourth of July and all that."

"Yeah, the carnival was the best place to be for fireworks. We used to sit outside our grandparents and watch them set 'em off over the lake. Then after all our sparklers were out, the parents would head out for the stage where someone would be singing. If they were real lucky an old member of *the Supremes* or a *Platter* and they'd rock out while we'd each figure out which ride we'd go on, since we had to choose one. Toni would always wait too long and then have to spend her tickets on candy. I usually picked something like the Tilt-A-Whirl or that one space machine thing that locked you in with twelve other people and spun you around 'til you flew up and down against the levels on the wall. It was only halfway over when we'd be begging them to stop. I remember never being able to stop laughing and your cheeks could hardly move because of the alternation of gravity. God, I loved that shit! It was like childhood in a bottle, times like that."

"Childhood in a bottle?" Kasey asked.

"Yeah, that's not exactly it, but it was like the crazies and the clowns, the games and the rides and the candy, hell that was the shit the O'Dell sisters wanted their lives to be filled with every day. I could eat caramel apples for breakfast lunch and dinner-"

"And cotton candy." Toni interjected with a sticky mouth and tongue covered in blue sugar dye.

"And cotton candy," I smiled back, "It's just that the first of the long trail of career dreams for me, had to be an acrobat, a strong woman, or even a roadie. The whole idea of keepin' on movin' and yet setting up the same everywhere we'd go seemed so strangely ethereal."

"Yeah, it's like you'd have this one big family that would know all the secrets behind all the fun, and god, you'd get to people-watch and have weekend romances you'd never see again because you'd be off to Kansas City, Chicago and the outskirts of New York," Toni said to the sky as she laid back on the bench to the left of us still throwing flecks of feathered blue cotton toward the back of her throat.

"It's like you'd hook up with the guy who worked the hammer and bell rig and throw him looks from with balloon pop, take breaks in the Haunted House and sleep at the back of the bus or even under the stars."

"With the bugs and the critters," Kasey laughed. "I never took either one of you two for romantics."

"I don't know if that part is as romantic as the shuffle of it all. I would just think that it would never get old. You'd sure have stories to tell, that's all I'm saying. We live in a world where you can't just stick your thumb out anymore. I can't even pick up an innocent looking twelve-year-old off the side of the road for the gun he might have in his Sanrio backpack. I just think *this* is it. This is where Jack and Bob stopped. This is were the celebration continues. It may be a little over-shattered by what stemmed from our childhood recollections, but it's still neon pink and flashing blue lights."

"They still got damn good cotton candy," Toni shouted.

I thought on whether or not I'd ever had any bad cotton candy and resigned that it really wasn't as good when bought at the grocery store.

"So you guys don't think that carnivals are becoming the malls of today?"

"Whadda ya mean?" Toni questioned Kasey.

"Well, you're starting to see 'em everywhere. They even set up in most mall parking lots and they're kinda the same in all the places," Kasey answered.

"I dunno if they're the same everywhere, but if they remind you at all of the last one, isn't that part of the charm? I go to a mall to shop, I go to carnival to have fun. At malls there's a shit-load of clothes I can't afford, at the circus there's lions and tigers and bears. At the mall, there's a greasy Chinese dive and if you're lucky *one* Orange Julius, but at the carnival there's pink popcorn and caramel apples?"

"And cotton candy," Toni interjected.

"And hot chocolate and cider," I continued, "The mall's always there, but the carnival only comes around twice a year. Here, we've got cover bands and country western singers, couples dancing in the dirt and kids laughing in sugar-shock. Nah, I don't think the carnival will ever become the mall. The carnival has been around too long to begin changing now."

"Yeah," Toni sighed as she got up from her bench and tossed her cotton candy paper center cone into the trash, "What kid didn't wanna run away with the circus?"

"The ones who hated candy and brushed their teeth without being asked," I answered.

"Well, who the hell ever wanted to join the rodeo?" Kasey asked.

"Probably every kid ever born in the South or with a cowboy hat and a toy gun," I said. I got up and walked with Toni back into the tent, forgetting to turn around to see whether or not Kasey was joining us, because at that point I really didn't have the energy to alleviate any further fears of the cow-ropers. Out in the Austin night heat of spring, with the bugs and dirt and the smell of churning hot candy in the vats of the vendors rolling wagons, I had grown dreary of defending the rodeo, the circus, and the carnival from its bad image. I just didn't see it deep in the heart of Texas. I couldn't rope a steer or hog-tie a pig, not because I plainly did not know how to, but because, yes, I would not have emotionally been able to capture an animal to the cheers of a meat-loving crowd of rodeo fans. But I sure relished my morning bacon, the McDonald's drive-through for my monthly double cheeseburger and my old pair of black leather boots. I knew Kasey didn't have a closet free of animal hide. What percentage of the world really did comply with the die-hard values of true animal activists? This is not to say I didn't believe that everyone had to do what they felt right, their little part, and you'd sure as hell never catch me in a fur coat. I might even cheer on those who pour red paint on the mink-clad ladies emerging from the opera, but I just didn't see the rodeo as the epicenter of animal rights sit-ins. Frankly, I wouldn't have even been there had Kasey not told Viv she wanted to 'do the Texas thing,' as she had put it. Sometimes, I think that living with the choices we have made, can be more important than standing against ourselves. I also have come to believe that you will only have as good of a time as you allow yourself and much of the stereotypes you see, have been painted onto the very landscapes that in fact, *you* brushed the paint upon.

I don't know what Kasey saw that night, but I had a pretty good idea from the resistance with which she was fighting the night and battling the good time that wanted to be had, that she had seen something that just *was not there*. At least it was not there for me. I saw cowboy boots and big black broad-rim hats, red bandannas and silver eagle belt buckles. I saw broad-shouldered men with spurs, hugging their wives and dancing with their girlfriends. I saw men in tight jeans with long braids buying dreamcatchers. Little kids ran about the petting zoo squealing as they attempted to touch the woolly sheep and moms took their pictures and laughed. A clown blew balloons and twisted them into hats. Girls grabbed their picks outta the bottom of their mini-fashion backpacks and quickly combed their sprayed bangs after exiting the Spider's Spinarama. The face-painter stuck her tongue out the side of her mouth as she arched the moon with perfection onto the side of a little cowboy's cheek. Screams rose up from inside the Haunted House and others undoubtedly from paranoid skinny women, envisioning themselves in their later years in the House of Mirrors. Maggie told us about the time her brother tried to ride a bucking bronco back in one of the Carolinas and Vivian listened with the intent of someone making up for her squeamish friend who had left the tent at the sight of the calf-roping.

We had come back in time for the singer. He was in fact the initial reason for coming, because even with all my convincing and rousing, Viv will never abandon her love of country music. I think that night, I may have enjoyed it more than usual, simply because I so *wanted* to have a good time and show others what it was like to do so. I recall Viv and Toni's and my motto, has always been, "*We could make a good time outta dancing in the back of my truck outside the Wash and Dry.*" Or something like that. That night though, we did not lack for stimulus. This wasn't a night in which we had to invent imaginary friends, talk to the birds or pretend we were professional bowlers at the Back Alley Lanes. This was the rodeo. This was the carnival. This was where magic often hovers like the ring around the full moon, flooding beams of stardust down to the revelers. And we reveled.

I think the carnival, the circus, the rodeo, hold so much magic, because they are among the last places where I would not be surprised to see just about anything. I believe that in *my* world, there is much fear. I walk down the street and am shocked by a man pissing on the side of a car. I walk through the park and am startled by a woman screaming at the trees. Down under the bridge, downtown, a family sleeps and on my way back from the club to my car someone sometimes follows me.

The carnival is different. All the things that normally shock me are contained and therefore calming. There are twenty port-a-potties against the wall. People are paid to scream at the circus, children shout out with glee as the baseball booth man hands them a big stuffed purple dinosaur that makes a noise when they squeeze its nose. Men can hardly contain their enthusiasm as little Billy Joe ropes his first steer and Rusty stays on the stallion at least five seconds. The rodeo is cheap, the carnival is practically free and everyone is the same, classless and comforted. We are safe. We sleep on benches and forget about the prospect of saving our teeth as we bite into our third caramel apple and reenter the fun house. Men are in leopard skin, big women wear tutus and children walk around with snakes around their carnie necks, but I am not afraid. There is nothing so strange I would not expect it here and that somehow provides me with an inexplicable sense of solace.

It is places such as these where I may feel most at peace, surrounded by cowboys and thespians, spinning wheels of light and bucking broncos, clowns and country western stars, the House of Mirrors and the big tent, big balloons and purple dinosaurs, aging sixties icons and men in tight blue jeans. It's the rodeo. It's the carnival. It's the last bastion of freedom. It's wild horses and Ferris wheels. It's Kerouac and Dylan. It can be Shakespearean and honky-tonk. It's Indians and cowboys. It's buying and selling, winning and losing, sweet and sour, dirty and clean, loud and laughable, sugary and hot, bright lights and the haunted night. It's on the road, traveling to a town near you, rolling away without apiece of Kasey, but with a little piece of me. It's in Austin, same place it'll be next year, same place we'll be next year and if not, I guess we'll have to catch it in Kansas City...

Mel McCabe

Heidi and the Reds

We waited inside that Starbucks across the street from the Texas souvenir shop on Congress. Everyone seems to know that trinket place. Hell, it's the only one in Austin, but it grows thin of fun after thirty minutes. Heidi's tardiness began to wear thin as well. Starbucks was beginning to think that I was stalking the cute blond-haired college guy with the pony-tail, which was an accusation for which I had once been guilty of back home. Nobody could blame me, they were brothers, tall and Greek and very publicly assessable. After two tall nonfat hazelnut lattes and a spell of sitting on their over-stuffed brown couch, Viv began to worry. I was only relieved that we had changed the meeting place from the street corner to inside the coffee place. Worry would have bled to irritation for me, mighty quickly, if I had had to stand on a corner forty-five minutes past a meeting time, for Heidi maybe not, but who the hell were these friends so necessary for her to bring anyway? I am not an anti-social or an abnormally bitchy young thing, not outside the guidelines of most California natives anyway, maybe for the typical Austinite, but nobody's *from* Austin.

Viv says to me back at the hotel, "Well, I don't know who these kids are. Heidi is just *really* paranoid about driving by herself. She saw some horrible accident awhile back when she was driving around Houston. There was blood and skin on the road and she kinda freaked out, so now she doesn't drive alone."

I peered through my mascara wand and replied, "That seems a little limiting, don't you think? I mean, isn't this the same chick who thrived off of traffic and wouldn't think of living any place where the cars weren't as packed up as the Santa Monica freeway? Plus, I can't even imagine not being able to jump in a vehicle and just drive off by myself. Some of the best thinking is done in the car by yourself."

Derrick continued to neatly and obsessively fold his dirty laundry. He agreed, "It does seem a little strange, but some people are affected differently by accidents. What are you talking about, her not wanting to live in a city without traffic though?"

I heard the blow dryer go off in the bathroom and leapt onto the bed with the channel changer, "Oh you haven't heard this one?"

"No, what?"

"When we all came out here to check out Texas for on vacation a few years back, Heidi's main gripe about Austin was its lack of traffic."

"You're kidding me."

"I shit you not. She had a year or two to go anywhere in Texas to gain residency before applying to schools and she chose Houston because of the traffic jams. She's a LA woman and figured nothing would make her more homesick than a town with an excellent freeway system and underpopulation."

Viv shouted out from the bathroom, "I didn't just hear you say, excellent freeway system, did I?"

"Okay, so the feeders suck shit here, but I can't even fathom Houston over Austin and you know it."

"I know, I know, it is molto bizarro, but she's the one moving back to California now and I'm sure it undoubtedly stems from all the beauty she's encountered in downtown Houston."

Another fifteen minutes on the couches at Starbucks and Derrick could no longer contain his hunger pangs, "Aren't you two hungry at all?"

Viv laughed and looked over at me with indifference, "You gotta just smack us when you wanna eat. George and I have adjusted to self-deprivation. Let's go back to the hotel and check and see if she's left a message and I have her number back at the room and I'll call her roommate, make sure she didn't get a late start or something."

We walked down Congress and around the corner to the car, "Do you know anything about these friends she's bringing?"

"Not really, I mean what was I supposed to ask her about them?"

"No, I'm just wondering if you happen to know their genders or relative ages or anything at all. I mean we *are* all packin' it into one hotel room tonight. I kinda like to know the dogs I'm lying with."

Viv cut over four lanes, spun around the turn around and merged from the feeder onto 35 before answering, "Well she mentioned that they were girls from work. I think they're from Russia or something, definitely Eastern Europe anyway."

"Do they speak English?"

"Look, I didn't get the whole low-down, I just know that they are Russian women from work. They could actually be why she is late. I mean, I don't know if they live anywhere near her so maybe she just took a long time picking them up."

"Yeah, well I'm not worried. I think that when people have a long distance to drive they always underestimate the time it's gonna take." I scooted up between the two front seats and turned toward Derrick, "So has Viv filled you in on the sleeping situation for tonight?"

"Whadda ya mean?"

I smiled and laughed as Viv caught my eye in the rearview mirror, "Well, we figured that we wanted no part of you playing the gentleman, and potentially sleeping on the floor when we are all paying for the room, so those three can share a bed and the three of us will be as snug as three bugs in another."

"Are you kidding?" Derrick laughed in his completely contagious manner, "There is no way the three of us are gonna fit in *one* bed."

"Hey that's not what the manager of the Econ-inn thought," exclaimed Viv as she changed lanes.

We all laughed in recollection of our warm welcome into the one star motel. I struggled to remove my last heeled leg from the extended seat belt determined to hold me prisoner at the back of the

Daihatsu. The rain pelted down and Viv held a
Chronicle over her head as Derrick just made a mad
dash into the office. None of us could decide who had
to check in, so that meant we all had to get out. The
Indian man behind the counter grinned as we spilled in
to the door. I noticed his son watching an episode of
Frasier in the lobby. I turned back to see the Indian
guy's potato-size bandaged finger holding out a
registration card with a pen. Viv, the responsible one,
and the man in our often used, false lesbian 'man-keep
away' pseudo act, signed in and handed the guy her
credit card. He looked up at the three of us, smiled and
in a giggly voice asked, "One bed?"

Derrick looked over at the two of us and began to
laugh uncontrollably as Viv and I simultaneously
shook our heads, "No." I bit my lip so hard in the
simple attempt to kill my need to laugh that Derrick
had to run out of the office to carry out his hysteria in
the glass middle room between the office and the
outside carport. Viv and I could not erase the silhouette
of his frame hunched over one knee laughing and
laughing to the point of busting a gut. The Indian man
just winked at Viv as if he seemed to truly believe that
even though he was turning over the keys to a two-bed
room, we would be sure to be only turning down one
bed that night. I rolled my eyes, Viv grabbed the keys
and we all went laughing off into the rain.

"So what you two are trying to tell me," Derrick
went on, "is that the three of them are all driving in
from Houston and kicking us all into one bed? I don't
think I would have felt obligated to sleep on the floor.
Two of them can hunker down on a good piece of
carpet if you ask me."

I looked over at Viv and began to laugh, "That's cool with me, as long as you're not gonna give them a mattress I have no problem telling them to hit the floor."

"Hell, I like Heidi, but we don't even know these other two," Derrick chimed in.

Viv looked back at me through the mirror once again and said, "Will you two stop planning everything? We haven't even met these people. We don't have to plan the whole evening."

"I know," I replied, "I'm just saying that if we don't have a tentative plan then all may be forgotten by the time we get back in the wee hours of the night and I don't want to make anyone uncomfortable and that way Heidi can figure out what she wants to do and all."

"Sometimes I think you have a 'tentative plan' for peeing. You need to take a pill and eat something. How much coffee have you had today anyway?"

"Only two cups."

"Two tall cups. Just stop rubbing your ear and everything will be fine. I swear to God, I'll just be happy once you've seen Tom and you can calm down."

Derrick looked over at Viv and asked, "What do you mean? Stop rubbing her ear?"

"Don't ask," I chirped.

"Oh, I'm shocked you haven't noticed, but George doesn't bite her nails like a normal anxiety freak. She just rubs her ear until she has to go to the doctor, whereupon he tells her that if she continues, she may give herself a Cancer abrasion that will have to be lasered off."

"That is such a scare tactic, who the hell ever heard of giving yourself Cancer from rubbing a body part? If that's the case Porn Stars would be dropping like flies, not to mention that Craig guy we used to go to high school with who spent more time in the bathroom than in class."

Derrick looked back, "Let me see."

I showed him my ear, that had developed a recent tic-tac size growth since the announcement of Tom Waits coming to town. Not being on schedule changed its color from red to black.

"That is disgusting!"

"Oh, go bite your nails! You know I went to elementary school with a girl who used to bite her nails so much that she went to Hawaii with her folks on vacation, bit her nails and ended up in the hospital."

Viv looked back again, "What on earth are you talking about?"

"She visited an inactive volcano and managed to get some of the lava particles stuck underneath her index finger. She bit into it a few days later and almost died, so who the hell is worried about Cancer?"

Viv snickered along with Derrick and shot back, "You're gonna end up with one ear twice the size of the other."

"Please, I can always have it pinned back, or pierced."

"Oh yeah, I've heard that's a mark of true beauty among some tribes in Africa."

"I've had worse ear problems than this before."

"Oh, yeah, Derrick I forgot to mention that when she pierced the inside of her ear, the tragus, she ended up with a growth the size of an almond."

"An almond?"

"Yeah," I rolled my eyes, "You know, an almond, the nut."

Derrick laughed and asked, "Well what did you do about it?"

"I named it."

"You named it?"

"Yeah," I took the metal out of course and found a friend, "Who was he again? Armand, the almond-shaped ear growth, that was him. I had to say goodbye to Armand about six months later though. He was a sick guy, couldn't exist in wellness, if you know what I mean."

"You are so strange," Vivian said.

"Oh, I find it wildly entertaining," commented Derrick.

"Well, thank you Derrick, because as long as I am being ridiculed, we must not forget to mention that I am not the one who is cool with our new communist friends sleeping on the floor."

"No, you're just the one who suggested the three of us sleep in *one* bed!" Derrick laughed.

"Hey, many a man would jump at the chance," Viv shouted.

"Please, they're not even paying, plus as you pointed out, they're Russian, it can't be as if they've never copped a squat on the floor for one night," Derrick mocked.

"Oh, Big Brother heard that one. KGB! KGB, come and get him! That's the way Viv and I are back to two in our bed," I yelled.

We all laughed as we pulled off on Sixth Street and parked it across the street from Maggie Mae's. Back up at the hotel, Heidi's roommate had told us that she had left at the crack of dawn and should have arrived hours earlier. There were no messages for us at the desk so we just gave her roommate Derrick's pager number and went to lunch. We still hadn't heard from Heidi by the time we got back to Congress and decided to check Starbucks one last time. Scheduled to go to the concert in the park at four thirty, we headed down to the old drugstore to purchase eats and drinks.

There's nothing quite like an Easter aisle at the drugstore. It sure as hell beats a Halloween or Christmas one and whoever thought the candy was better in October than March was never a chocoholic. Maybe it's just a girlie thing, but Eckhert had a pastel explosion running three aisles and I threw Derrick the camera and made Vivian humor me by dancing around with the rolls of pink, yellow, baby blue and mint green cellophane wrapper. Viv threw one up in the air in classic majorette style and I watched it unsuccessfully crash to the floor. We decided to quickly make our candy selections before being escorted from the premises. I shoved the Bird Eggs, Bridge Mix and assortment of Cadbury mini's and cream filled eggs into my backpack and we tied our sweaters around our shoulder in that wretched yuppie 'cell-phone in the pocket' fashion as Viv took pictures down Congress of us posing like freaks. By the time we made it back up to the coffee shop I suggested we cross on over to *The Paramount* to see what time the Tom was playing. It was sold out, which was a discovery that caused more pain to my heart than most news of death, but all was not for naught as Heidi was standing there with the Reds right on the other side of the red carpet. I recognized her immediately and smiled at the thought of our luck. Viv would have walked right past her had Derrick and I not yelled out, which proves more funny if you would know that this girl is *her* ex-roomie from LA and we had only met her but a few times. Vivian is always the one trying to convince me that she is *so* much better with faces than with names, although she *is* massively better at recollecting just about anything when compared to a name.

Heidi didn't look all that different from the last time I had seen her, which was just about two years prior to the day. We had all ventured out from California in the attempt to grasp onto some part of Austin that could pull each of us away from the ocean and into the tumbleweeds, cactus, bugs and humidity. I recall Vivian had believed that it was going to take no convincing to erupt Heidi from her life in LA as the two of them had common ulterior motives, getting into school and claiming residency to do so. It was only a matter of picking a city to complete the plan. Research had been conducted and Austin was chosen as the safest bet at cajoling a Californian out of her bubble of a near utopian existence in San Francisco. The troubles that lie are usually done in mistaking the mind of a Southern Californian and her needs as paralleling anywhere within the realm of a Northern Californian. Despite Vivian's five-year stint in LA, her new roots did not run as deep as her homegrown San Franciscan ones and she stuck to Austin as quickly as the bats cling daily to the bottom of the south bridge. I know she was as shocked, as I was when I threw my stake in the land, but no questions were asked and we ran with it. Heidi ran further east and drove her little pickup out to Houston with another college friend, planning as she later told us in the park, "Never to really live there. I mean, I always knew, I was going back to California. Texas just isn't for me."

Well of course it wouldn't be. I mean when you 'always' know something, you're never gonna give the possibility half a chance. "Viv, didn't you think it was weird, when Heidi said she *always* knew she was going back home?" I asked as we drove down Guadalupe in search of a versateller.

"Yeah, but she's so LA, I'm not surprised. I mean she has her boyfriend back in San Jose now too."

"I know but when she came out here he was living in Ohio and I just think it's odd that she never gave Texas a chance, don't you?"

"Well, ya. I mean I could never live my life thinking every day about being somewhere else. The fact that she chose Houston simply because it reminded her more of LA and didn't come out to Austin even though she would have had a blast, just shows that she was determined not to have fun."

Derrick looked over at Viv with a glance of disbelief, "You mean you don't think she *wanted* to have fun?"

I leaned back into the middle of the seat and Viv shot me a 'put your seatbelt in my twenty pound car' look, "I love Heidi dearly, I mean what I know of her, but I just think that this whole move was all about a means to an end and if you ask me, you can look at your whole fuckin' life as a means to an end, but there is no way I'm gonna *live* it that way. If anyone asked me three years ago if I thought I'd be happily living in the heart of Texas and thinking of raising a familia out here I'd laugh in his face, but here I am."

Derrick laughed, "So you could see yourself out here forever?"

Viv chimed in, "What's forever? Get a grip, there's no way that girl could live out here without me and with the bugs, but if she shells out for one of those two hundred dollar electronic roach killer contraptions then I could sing another tune."

I smiled and thought of myself killing a bug with my bare hands and shuttered, "Let's face it, there's no ocean, no good shoe stores, no professional sports teams, and not too many men with English accents either, but hell Tom blows into town once every twenty years and with my own private plane I could hunker down on a nice piece of ranch land, y'all."

Vivian quickly determined that I was not just hugging a random girl walking down Congress and recognized her as indeed being Heidi. I shook hands with the Reds, who were introduced as Alex and Katia. Derrick and Viv and I drilled Heidi for a good ten minutes on why the hell she was so late, as it had been a lapse of four hours off the projected meeting time. Katia's car had broken down halfway to Austin so they had to be towed back to Houston and then give it a go in Alex's car. They had left us a message at the desk of the Econ-inn, but go figure with the more than quirky one bed pushing Indian guy, we had not received it, even when we had gone back and directly asked the man. She had told the guy that our new meeting time would be better at four in front of *The Paramount* and who would have guessed we would meet just at that place and time without even having received the message? I quickly realized that I had to tone down the high speed Valley talk of normal yesteryear as the Russians were only able to understand about half of the questions I directed toward them, which is more than the average slow drawled Texan often does. We told Heidi and the Reds to go on up to their car and that we'd pull back down around and have them follow us to the park. I was more than relieved that we had already eaten as they had as well and poor Derrick would have been at the 'scrape himself off the cement' status had we deprived him of yet another meal for the weekend.

Munching on Bird Eggs back to the car, we admitted to poor timing on meeting up if only because my own state of panic had set in due to the status on the Tom concert. Viv solved all problems as the eternal level-headed one and suggested we drop them off at the park, show them a good spot to hang out, so we'd know where to meet up with them and then we'd all head off to obtain money and track down ticket-sellers and scalpers. When we pulled down by the Capital building, where they were parked, Alex was changing pants. This proved to be a good thing, because had the pant change not been made so early in our meeting, I might have never discovered Alex was in fact a man.

"Alex is a dude!" I exclaimed rather loudly as Viv quickly rolled up her window, shushed me and started in on the hysterical laughing perpetuated by none other than Derrick. "Well, why the hell didn't you two tell me?" I exclaimed in an irritated, butt of the joke kind of way.

Viv turned around as she pulled up on the e-brake and mocked me through veiled laughter and a wave of acknowledgment to Heidi, "Well what the hell were Derrick and I supposed to say? Hey, George, I know you are delirious in your panicked state of potential Tom-withdrawal, but as you pop that Kava Kava, notice that the blond Russian has a penis!"

Derrick laughed harder which set me into a snort, "I thought you said that Heidi's friends were both female!"

Derrick mocked me further, "Let me get out and tell Alex that he is not following the itinerary and if he could just Bobbitize than we could go on as planned. I think the further kink lies in trying to get the three of them in one bed as the two of you are trying to get me."

"Ha, ha," I scoffed, "You have to admit that in a 1940's Eastern European, hearty stock of Germany, kind of way, Alex could look like a woman."

"I don't think so," the two shouted back in heavy stereo.

After Alex finished zipping up his chinos, we motioned for them to follow us down to Waterloo. We parked it and walked across the street to find ourselves more than a little early to no true despair since they had showed up so late, if even they had left a message. The Reds seemed a little out of it as to why we were quickly exiting the park after having just gotten there, but once we showed them the fajitas stand and the bathroom, appeared pacified enough to care very little of our disappearance. We returned an hour later, still ticketless yet with more hope of regaining respiration later on that night. By five, the park had filled to almost eight thousand and we found Heidi standing on a bench looking for us with her hand to her forehead.

Alex and Katia were laying down relaxing and performing an adequate job of saving us a few spots. Vivian sat down next to Heidi and the two of them began to make up for time with medical application scare stories. Derrick and I took a stab at conversing with Alex.

"So Alex," I began, "Where exactly are you from in Russia?"

He mumbled the name of a city of which I had never heard.

"How long have you been in the states?"

"Almost two years now."

"Are you working with Heidi?"

"No, I am friends with Katia, but I am going to graduate school in Houston."

I truly hated this form of one sentence questioning, one-sentence responses, but once you begin this shit you can only hope that one sentence will eventually graduate into the paragraph level where the pain of thinking up new anal first time meeting questions will cease. I always most definitely choose to go back to the one sentence answers when the questions begin to come hurled in my direction, of course always at the "What do you do for a living?" state.

This is not a harmful question, nor an uncommon one, but wouldn't you just love it if you could meet people and for the entire first night have it be absolutely forbidden to ask them what they did for a living or even any of the old tired questions? We could bypass all the haggard old conversations regarding career plans all directed at getting to how much money you make, what kind of car you drive, how much you pay for your apartment, where you went to school, etc,

etc. Instead, we could get poetic and ask about the greatest moment in your life, the funniest thing you ever did and your favorite Halloween costume. Where you could be at that moment if you could close your eyes and teleport your body somewhere else. Explain the plot of your life. Explain the plot in the greatest book you ever read. The best movie you ever saw? Who did you see it with? Who was your childhood best friend? Why are you no longer friends with him? What do you normally do on Saturday nights? On Monday nights? Have you ever thought of killing yourself? Killing someone else? Killing your pet? Your clock? How'd you spend your twenty-first birthday? Do you believe in God? gods? The Goddess? And afterlife? Reincarnation? Do you think you're gonna make it to heaven? On your way to hell? Have you ever had cybersex or opened another person's mail? God, gods, and Goddess, I'd love it.

"So what do you do for a living?" Alex asked.

"I work part-time for a small publishing company and full-time at writing and trying to get my shit published." I smiled as Derrick looked away, undoubtedly planning how to explain his position as a Consultant Analyst in terms for the cosmonaut to comprehend. This is not said with a shred of bitchiness because I have had Derrick's job explained to me at least half a dozen times and still have no clue what it is that he does to explain his own phone line and secretary.

"Really? That is goot. Will you be published soon?"

This was the point in the conversation where I must choose to either bullshit, give the naïve listener the low-down on the two percent of writers who have an agent or a little of both with much defense piled on top. "Well, I'm still trying to find an agent. That's had to take a backseat though, since I have been doing a lot of writing as of late. You either find yourself devoting your time to writing, writing, writing or you let that slide and spend all your time trying to get an agent and have your work seen."

"Yeah, I heard it very difficult to get agent. In Russia, we have better writers so it is not so difficult to get published."

"Really?" I smirked, "Well when I first met you I thought you were a girl," I found myself saying out loud.

Derrick began to choke on a Bird's Egg.

Alex ignored my comment and smiled, "So what exactly are those books that you have wrote about?"

"Well," I struggle to decide which tact to take to interest the young male foreign audience. It becomes more difficult to parallel your work to other books when you wonder what sort of literature a student in communist Eastern Europe grew up reading, "I don't know if you're familiar with *Catcher & the Rye* or *Basketball Diaries*? I guess loosely, my first novel is a female take on the combo. It's a narrative of a girl growing up with eleven close friends, their bouts with drinking, drugging, finding themselves and the likes." Alex nods although that means nothing because he has been nodding since we met and I thought him a woman, which was undoubtedly when I could really read him. I continue, "The second work, is a story loosely based on Vivian's and my travels around the United States. A story about people in their twenties deciding whether or not to buck the corporate system and where exactly they might find their niche in the world. I also have a book of poems, which I am sure will hit the bestseller's list any day since poetry is wildly appreciated by young Americans as you may well know and right now I am writing a book of short stories."

Derrick turned from the stage and smiled over at Alex, "You never know Alex, you could very well wind up in one of George's books. I'm always on the sly as to what I say."

Alex gave a disbelieving grin reminding me how much I hated going off on my future career exploits, although I supposed I had taken the wrong choice in life aspirations if I was already uncomfortable talking about myself. Then again, what the hell was an agent for? I scarfed down a few dozen Bird's Eggs, offering some to Alex and Katia which of course they refused with two, 'look at the American girl eat like shit' looks. I would have even found myself possibly polishing off the bag had not Derrick confiscated them for his own enjoyment and then began sharing them with the hacky-sac players in the circle next to us, only in Austin.

Vivian and Heidi looked up from their corner and I took the opportunity to ask Heidi all the questions I was sure Vivian had just asked her. I was far too curious about her move back to California to hold it in.

The next band came out and Derrick and the Ruskies stood up to look. Derrick's mock country cowboy dance was too funny to control my laughter as completed the look with a little hay (with which they had carpeted the wet lawn) between his teeth in addition to his galloping pony dance to the accordion player's solos. If the Russians had not been able to digest the toilet mouth sugar beast, Derrick was no consolation to normalcy.

"So what's up Heidi? I heard you're moving back?" I asked.

"Yeah, I'm doin' okay. I just reallllly do not like Houston. I am so excited to move back."

"So you're going back to LA?"

"No, I'm gonna move up to San Jose with Jeff."

"And you're movin' in with him then."

"Yeah, I'm gonna look for my own place, but I figure that could take awhile so I'll move in with him first."

I thought to myself, why look for another place when you are essentially moving to an area to be *with* someone. I am usually counted among the irate breast-heaving feminists, but when you have no job and know nobody and are moving somewhere to be *with* someone, am I right in assessing that you are getting hitched? I cut to the quick, "So do I hear wedding bells or what?"

"Yeah, I think so. I mean I love Jeff, but we've never really lived with one another and we have been doing the long distance thing for years now so I'm just afraid it's gonna be really difficult seeing one another all the time now when we haven't been used to it."

This I could see if they had not been going out before she moved. But in reality, I had had great exposure to the long-distance relationship via Vivian's love-life and banked on Heidi's ear being plastered to the phone to hear Jeff's panting, "I love you and miss you soooo much sweetie," at least five times a day.

This is often more than one gets in the close proximity of waking up in the same bed each morning next to their shit for breath. "You guys talk on the phone all the time don't you?"

"Oh, God, George, you should see the phone bills."

"Well, I'm sure you guys'll be fine then."

"What about you? How's the man status?"

"Heidi, nothing's changed for me. I mean I just wrote two books and am workin' on the third so of course I don't have a man."

"George, you just don't give anyone a chance."

Oh, yes, poor manity, they are screaming for George to throw them a bone. Of course my reasoning falls on deaf ears. I mean why the hell doesn't George have a man? Who gives a shit that the chick has a goal, a dream, the incessant need to get these words the fuck outta her head, she isn't filling her hole, that vast void that must exist since she has not had a man in soooo long. Please! "Well, you're probably right, I've haven't really given anyone opportunity, but if I had to devote half my life taking care of someone else, I'd be left with the other half of myself falling to pieces."

Heidi smiled a weak grin of a soon-to-be-married woman who would undoubtedly feel it her duty to throw the bouquet in my direction and say her love prayers at night for me. Viv nodded at my perfectly practiced speech losing its enthusiasm and vigor in my own lack of believability in its content. "So when you movin' back?"

"Next month, I really wish I woulda gotten more of a chance to come out and visit you two. I can hardly believe that we were so close, all in Texas and hardly saw one another in years."

"I know, it's a trip," I thought to myself as I recalled Viv visiting up in Houston and relaying that she would never take me because I might suffocate upon the pollution and kill the bad drivers with vulgarity for which they would never have heard cast from the mouth of a red lipstick donned woman.

Back at the car Derrick had asked, "Do you two think that you would have had such a good time with Heidi out here too?"

"Hell yeah," we both shot back.

"If Heidi had come out here we would have all gotten a house with a yard and a dog and had backyard barbecues. It would have been the heaven we had, but even better." I exclaimed.

Derrick looked back and forth from Viv to me with quizzical eyes, "So you're just talkin' property then? I don't know if you two would have remained so close."

"Please Derrick!" Viv shot back, "George and I are family, you don't become any less close when you're family, you just *are*. With Heidi here, it woulda just been a whole 'more the merrier' scenario, but oh well, we all make decisions for certain reasons and George and I didn't suffer any the more for it."

"Oh yeah. Screw it, no skin off my back. I just think Heidi would have been singin' a different song had she moved to Austin." I thought out loud.

The Reds got up from our circle in the hay and Katia announced that she and Alex were going to go and take a walk, the first words I had heard her utter since the muffled hello hours earlier. When they had departed a distance of at least ten feet, I asked Heidi if the two were together, almost assuming the 'yes' answer before it came out of her mouth. Instead, she told us that they weren't and that Alex was actually a friend of Katia's boyfriend or another friend back in Russia. (Don't think this is foreshadowing as to either Viv or I gettin' nasty with Alex. I'd have rather opted for the Indian guy back at the Travel Lodge.) We all got up for *The Gords*, Derrick continuing to embellish upon his galactic cowboy routine while Viv, Heidi and I all swayed to the drums until the Communists returned.

"We walked down to Sixth Street," Katia announced as they found their way back to our collapsed hay spot. Viv and I shot each other looks of shock. Our ability to walk great lengths had ended after two months in the humid temperatures of the Southwest and we laughed on the inside that we were returning to where they had just come minutes from now for vittles and jowl chomping. It was not hard to tell that Derrick was once again hungry, a fact I should not make sound 'out of the norm,' since Viv's and my food habits were in fact eschewed from the norm of most of the country.

We all waited in the parking lot for Viv to go and get the car. Derrick and I clasped our arms over our chests in unsuccessful attempts to hide the uncomfortable feeling of having nothing to say to the Reds. I asked Katia how she had chosen Houston as her destination in the States from Russia and she retorted with a curt, "Why not?" which solidified the question of whether we were dealing with a language barrier or a bitch barrier.

In the car, I relayed the response to Viv as Alex followed us back to Sixth Street, honking whenever he felt Viv was going too slow (a concept Viv was having a serious problem with because whenever she attempting to speed up to five below the speed limit we would nearly lose him).

"Well I thought Alex seemed nice when we were chatting with him on the lawn," Derrick claimed as Alex beeped his horn.

"I agree wholeheartedly," I told him, "But there was definitely a little something off, especially regarding the 'there are so many great writers in Russia' comment and the dubious glance at my likelihood of getting published. And I'm not even really criticizing Alex here, the only real problem I have with him is the fact that I may never fully be able to erase seeing the outward shape of his tighty-whities when I was convinced that boy was a woman man. My gripe's with that Katia."

"Well," Viv cut in, "It is reallly odd that she was so curt in saying she had no reason for coming out to Texas because she told me that her father lived in Houston and that was the real reason she ended up there."

"How odd," Derrick and I said together. "Let's just lose 'em around the next bend. It could be an honest mistake." Derrick laughed.

Vivian surprised us by responding, "Okay."

She put the pedal to the medal, made two quick rights and a left, ducked into a covered parking lot and they were nowhere to be seen. The three of us piled out of the car and scooted up Congress, only to round the corner where Heidi and the Reds could be seen walking right toward us.

"Damn," I whispered.

"We thought we had lost you," Heidi laughed nervously.

"Where are we gonna eat?" Viv asked as if I had any idea what the Ruskies wanted. All that drastically stuck to my mind of my trip to St. Petersburg as a teenager was really nothing more than lard and tomatoes, tomatoes and lard, I banked on these kids eating anything if *I* could live off lard for three weeks.

We walked down Sixth Street and by the third menu we had looked at, and memorized, the Reds could not find anything palatable. Derrick shot us a look of surprise. We continued to saunter down the sidewalk as the street filled up with each passing minute. I was beginning to think that the food situation must have drastically changed in the Soviet Union since the fall of communism, but believed that even Parisian food critics would have found something amenable on the menu of the last place we had passed up. By the time we got down to The Iron Cactus, Viv's suggestion, due to the terrific view with the roof seating, the Reds spent ten minutes examining the menu before halfway nodding looks of slight approval. Walking upstairs, we were told it would be an hour wait and I knew that was hardly feasible. I did not have an hour worth of banter to deliver and was already getting nervous as to how much time I wanted to spend away from the theater where I needed to wrestle down a scalper for the ticket to my show. In the downstairs dining room the wait was only twenty minutes. We slugged off to a table by the bar where Alex and Katia went and got some wine, finding their way back to the table to amuse themselves for a 'goot' five minutes on the electronic red light pager that was supposed to go off when our table was ready. As much as I had made no secret to Derrick just how ridiculous I thought his own company computer pager was, I shot up a doozy of a prayer to the Goddess for the fascination in which it held the Reds. Time passed more quickly than it had in hours as everyone took a turn emailing a friend from Derrick's pocket and listening to the explanation of its ability to call anyone in the country with the sound of an electronic voice.

The food was good, the conversation to no shock lacking and probably due much in part to me, as I had grown tired of trying to find a commonality between us. To speak with only Derrick proved to be somewhat excluding, but after the Reds resorting to talking in Russian, that proved to be just what I did. Viv managed to sum up the remains of the years that had not been expelled in the park to Heidi and looked somewhat sad at the thought of probably never seeing her old college roommate again.

I asked Viv later as we were walking past the outdoor 'pizza by the slice' place, "So you think you and I will be able to wind up the years in one afternoon after we've gone our separate ways and haven't spoken in a few years."

Derrick laughed, "Yeah, right, you two not talking!"

Viv looked over at me and smiled, "I know you have this melodramatic concept of just slipping off to London in the middle of a lease, but I find it hard to imagine even if we did go years without talking, reuniting to have you with nothing to say at the end of only one afternoon, not to mention you're not rid of me, for the way I see it, at least the next four years."

"That's right I forgot we are talking to the mistress of disappearance here. I still can't believe the way you leave without telling people where you are going," Derrick laughed.

"Hey, when old friends, if so you wish to call them, call up the folks' house, my mother resigns to telling them I'm living in the deep South, a rodeo rider without a phone number."

Derrick questioned, "How does Viv have your number for the next four years though?"

"She co-signed my car, the car I'll realistically be making payments on 'til senior- citizendom. I guess I'm destined to remain without a good disappearing act 'til at least then."

After dinner, we separated, a concept that I believe truly allied us with the assholes of the world, or so the Reds made us believe with their less than complacent glances. Viv gave Heidi the newspaper clipping that displayed all the clubs. I circled the ones I believed they'd have the best chance of getting into. They didn't have wristbands and on the last night of the festival some of the spots might have been harder than others. I told Viv and Derrick it wouldn't be worth it for them to go to a club that would let Heidi and the Reds in because their wristbands would be worthless for the night. They walked me up to *The Paramount*, got me a ticket after much finagling and ended up down at *Antone's*.

We had agreed to all meet down at the Cuban coffee spot down on Lavaca just after two, figuring that if they had not been able to get in anywhere, they could rest their dogs to some good ol' acoustic music outside and drown their exhaustion in some damn good chai. They were nowhere to be found when I arrived at about two thirty, neither were Derrick and Vivian so I floated back up to *Antone's* where I could hear the horns of *The Scars* through the open door. I pushed my way to the front. One often finds herself justified to shove and grind her breasts among a quite drunken and sometimes rowdy crowd when she needs to get someone's attention and in fact meet up with her remaining party. I listened to the last of their set, focusing as always upon the bassist, not because *The Scars'* bassist is a piece of eye candy, realistically the guy is adorable but comes up to my knees, but because the bass holds much intrigue for me. As the bar lit up to let everyone out, it became a medal-winning task, to avoid slipping on a rolling bottle.

It was as hot outside as inside. Viv asked on the way down to the car, "Do you guys wanna go back to the motel?"

"No way," I retorted. "I already checked Ruta Maya and they weren't there, so they must be back there, but I'm famished and wanna talk."

They both agreed. We ended up on Kerbey Lane, at a table within the half hour. After a lengthy dinner, or if you wanna call it breakfast of enchiladas, chicken quesos and pasta, we found ourselves sitting in the parking lot of the Econ-inn, not wanting to go inside.

"Viv, what the hell are we gonna do? I need to sleep with the TV on!" I whimpered.

"So sleep with the TV on! I don't give care what anybody says," Viv shot back and made a move to get out of the car, whereupon Derrick pulled her back inside.

"You can't get out," I said.

"Well, why not?" asked Viv.

"Because," I shot back, "As soon as you get into the room you can't talk to us anymore so you have to think of anything you might wanna say before you are banished into silence."

Viv looked over at me and then Derrick, "I recognize that to be an inconceivable event, not-speaking for hours, for you, but some of us call it sleep and it is five in the morning. I think I'm gonna be able to handle it."

"Let's go bowling," Derrick exclaimed.

"Okay," I smiled thinking I was never going to be able to sleep without *MTV* or at least *Nick at Night*, not to mention who knew how the sleeping arrangement was to be set. "Oh crap, I don't have any socks!"

"So, just bowl without socks," Derrick naively suggested.

"This, coming from someone who folds his dirty laundry?" I said, "Do you have any idea how easily one can obtain athlete's foot from bowling shoes with no socks! That is just nasty."

Viv backed me up, "She's right, but we could go in and get socks."

"Oh, hell if we have to *go in* we might as well just *stay in*, plus I know you have to get up and write three papers tomorrow, or today, so let's just go in," I said to Viv.

We spent another good ten minutes in the car just laughing and determining who was going to brush their teeth first since there was to be very little speaking once inside, or so I suggested even though Viv and Derrick could have given a rat's ass as to their decorum among the sleeping Heidi and the Reds.

We walked to the room and I asked, "Do you think they went home early or just forgot about meeting us?"

Viv turned and said, "I'm sure they just went back to the room early."

Inside, the Reds were already lying on the floor, looking quite cozy indeed for a non-couple, couple. They had moved the table and chairs over into the corner, unfortunately on top of our bags and we each took turns twisting and contorting our bodies around the immovable table (as their feet lay inches away from the edge) in attempts to find clothes in which to sleep. Viv brushed her snags first, leaving Derrick and I outside to suppress our laughter from the sound my Velcro shoes made after removing them. I desperately wanted to take a shower but thought better of the noise and the fact that it was nearing the hour of six and the others would be awake soon, depending on when they had arrived back at the room.

After changing, I managed to bypass the floor obstacles into bed even with the lights already flicked off. An easy task is not made of falling asleep to the sound of your stomach digesting three spicy enchiladas, half a plate of baked beans, four cups of coffee and an evening of Tom Waits. I began to drift off as Viv and Derrick started in on their series of undiluted bellows of laughter that definitely woke one of the Ruskies and prevented me from joining. I was on the other side of Heidi and knew that my body had no capability of laughing without shaking and therefore waking her out of her deep slumber. I shushed them a dozen times to no avail, tried to rip the channel changer in the dark from its glued status to the bedstand with which I had intending on hurling at the insensitive jokesters and resolved to slide into my dreams where Tom and another plate of enchiladas were already waiting.

Viv and I awoke at a ridiculously early hour, despite those who were even earlier to bed. After going to the bathroom to find the toilet seat up and piss all over the pot and the floor, I deduced that it could have only been our dear friend Alex. Derrick wouldn't dare think to leave the seat up even in the wee hours of a stuttered slumber. I thought the floor piss was a particularly pleasant touch and spent my first morning moments wiping up the cold blue tiles, the rest of the toilet seat and then disinfecting my hands for five minutes with half a bar of soap. Heidi was already awake when I got out and Katia made a lunge for the bathroom where the sound of the shower could be heard thirty seconds later.

I sat back down on the bed. Viv propped herself up on a pillow as I turned toward Heidi, "So where'd you guys end up going last night?"

"Well," she whispered and leaned over so that Alex wouldn't hear, "they really didn't wanna stay anywhere. We started out where *Sister 7* were playing, but they hated that so I ventured into the entrance of a few other places before we actually paid and they didn't wanna go there either so we hiked down to the Music Hall for Jimmie Vaughn."

Viv sat up, "How was that?"

"Well, *I* had a good time, but when we got there the second act had cancelled so we had to wait almost an hour before he came on and then they wanted to leave pretty soon after that."

My eyes widened and I looked back over at Viv with a shocked face, "You're kidding! What time did you guys get outta there, or back here?"

"Well we headed out of the Music Hall at about two and were back here about quarter after."

I was shocked and asked, "So you guys were just too tired to head on over to Ruta Maya?"

She looked over in the direction of Alex who had begun to stir and mouthed the words quietly, "They didn't wanna go."

Viv and I turned toward one another and met with identical bizarre glances. Derrick woke up as Katia came out of the bathroom. Heidi asked if we all wanted to go to breakfast with a plea in her voice. I recognized that as little time as I wanted to spend with Alex and Katia, I did feel bad that Heidi had been stuck with the wet noodles for the whole evening prior and that we realistically might likely never see her again. "Sure, let's go to breakfast," Viv nodded as she looked for affirmation from Derrick and I and we quickly looked away.

Heidi checked Alex and Katia to find two blank stares of people who were not going to pretend that they wanted to spend another second with the likes of us. Alex stared all of us into getting ready at MACH speed and my much-needed shower from the night before, took its place and title as the much-needed shower for the afternoon. Derrick, Vivian, Heidi and I all went inside to check out and try and discover just what had happened to the message Heidi had relayed the morning before. I sat down next to the Indian's guy kid, now watching a *Designing Women* rerun and rummaged through my makeup bag. All the mascara, lipstick and liner from my purse only heightened the look of weary and worn already plastered to my mug.

The kid on the couch jumped up and ran over to the window when we all heard a loud crash outside. The Indian guy, Derrick, Viv, Heidi and I ran out the door to see Vivian's Daihatsu smashed squarely into the bumper of an old Mercury parked in the manager's spot. Alex was behind the wheel and Katia lay face down in the backseat.

Derrick began to laugh uncomfortably and I followed suit. Heidi stood shocked and red-faced. Vivian ran over to the driver's side window and began to yell at Alex, "What are you doing?"

"Trying to drive away," Alex responded matter-of-factly.

Derrick and I gave each other quizzical glances before continuing to laugh harder.

"Where were you going?" Vivian yelled.

"Back to Houston," Alex said. Katia lifted her head up from the backseat and refused to look anyone in the face.

"But my car is a piece of crap!" Vivian yelled back.

"It is better than mine," Alex said.

The Indian guy ran over beside Viv, opened the car door and yanked Alex out. "You are going to have to pay for my car!" he screamed.

"I don't have insurance," Alex told him.

"You are still paying!" the Indian guy yelled.

Vivian backed the Daihatsu out from the Mercury's bumper and we discovered there was very little damage. Knowing that Alex was never going to pay and just wanting to get out of there fast, Heidi retrieved her bag from Alex's car and wrote the manager a check for three hundred bucks. He seemed pacified and she handed Viv check as Derrick and I climbed back into Viv's car and Alex and Katia into their's.

"What's going on?" I asked Vivian as she got back into the car and Derrick tried to stifle his snicker.

"Let's just get this breakfast over with," Vivian responded.

I put my head in between their seats and asked, "We are still going to eat with them? I don't wanna spend another second with those Reds. I don't think Heidi does either."

Derrick looked back, "I thought you said you weren't gonna make trouble for the next two years after having seen Tom?"

"I lied. I'm not *trying* to make trouble, but do you really wanna conversate with those two over fluffy eggs and perfectly good coffee?"

Derrick lamented, "No, but it's a good excuse to go back to Kerbey Lane."

"Oh, let's not take them all the way down there and then spoil our favorite spot on top of it," I pleaded.

"Oh, we'll go to the one up north," Viv compromised as she turned around the feeder and onto the freeway. We dropped Derrick off in front to see how long the wait was and he came back to inform us that it was at least an hour.

I popped my head out the window and yelled, "IHOP is right down the street, let's go there." I truly loved IHOP pancakes more than any other food on the planet. It was the strangest thing, but two years prior, pancakes had done nothing shy of making me wretch, but I woke up one morning and *had* to have them, went on over to IHOP and scarfed down half a dozen. My sister went on to work at IHOP and even after the discount and added information as to the pancakes being frozen, I still never got sick of those flappers with that strawberry syrup.

Alex peeked his head out the other side of the car and yelled, "Where is Denny's? I want to go to Denny's."

Derrick put his head in his hands so as not to be seen by the other car and began to laugh which sent me into hysterics and left Viv biting her lip, "Alex, I don't know where there's a Denny's. George have you got any idea?"

I knew that when Viv resorted to asking the Queen of the directionless and memory dysfunction she was only seconds short of getting ready to lose it. "I think there is actually one downtown near that old closed-down grill. Member we went there with Matt and Toni?"

Viv turned around like she was gonna smack me and said, "No, I have no idea what you are talkin' about."

"Okay, well I don't know then."

Derrick began to laugh harder and Viv shouted out, "Alex, we're going to IHOP!" She peeled out of the Kerbey Lane parking lot and Alex began to beep his horn in some sort of incredibly uncommunistic protest. "This kid is bugging the crap outta me," Viv whined which made us laugh harder.

"All I have to say," Derrick chimed in, "Is who the hell knew there was a difference between IHOP and Denny's?"

"Dessert," Viv and I said in unison.

"Really?" Derrick inquired, "Who has the better dessert?"

"Well," Viv said as she pulled into the IHOP turn, "On our road trips we've probably hit more IHOPs and Denny's than any other non-trucking Americans and IHOP may win in the pancake department according to the hotcake connoisseur back there, but Denny's takes the cake with their Reese's pie."

"Yeah, their Oreo Cookie one too," I yawned back, "Now, are you gonna get out and see how long the wait is or what?"

Derrick rolled his eyes and Viv and I waited in the car, "Viv?"

"What?"

"I pray the wait is long and then we can tell Heidi that we have to get going back home and say goodbye here."

"And eat downtown."

"Exactly," I laughed, "And eat downtown."

We watched Derrick as he came out of the IHOP in slow motion with the news to deliver, did we or did we not get to cut the cord now?

"Two hour wait. I'm gonna go tell Heidi," Derrick told us with a look of glum consternation.

Viv hopped out of the car and Derrick ran toward Alex and for the first time the whole trip I floated out the back without getting caught on the seatbelt with shear speed and determination. Viv and I plastered sad looks upon our excited and relieved faces and took a few last pictures with Heidi before shaking hands with the Reds and watching our old friend drive off forever. As we turned back toward the Daihatsu we heard Alex's car honking, saw the first smiles on the Reds' faces as they turned and waved, and heard them shout out, "Hope you get published, George!" It never fails to amaze me how the implication of fame changes people, turns assholes into born-again Christians and Communists into Capitalists. We shot back into the car and Derrick began to laugh.

"What's so funny?" I asked.

"Yeah, what the hell are you laughing at now?" Viv inquired.

"It's only a thirty minute wait, but I couldn't take the chance that you guys would make us stay there with them and there was no way I was gonna wait for even ten minutes with those two. I feel bad for Heidi, but *they tried to steal our car*!"

I began to laugh and Viv laughed harder, "I love you Derrick! Thank you, thank you, thank you!" Viv screamed.

I caught Viv's eye in the rearview mirror as she peeled out onto 35 and asked her and Derrick, "Why do you guys think they hated us?"

"I have no clue," said Derrick.

"I don't think they *hated* us," retorted Viv with a voice of indifference, "Although it could have been those Ruskie vibes you kept sending off. Maybe they sensed your fear of Big Brother and secretly detested Derrick for his capitalistic computer pager."

"I'm sure!" I exclaimed as the wind began to whip around the back with the windows both rolled down, "They obviously disliked *you* the most, since they tried to steal *your* car! The funny thing is that they probably aren't Communists anyway, since they wanted so badly to come to America and all. Those are the people who are totally capitalistic. America is the biggest

Communist country of all anyway. I love Communists, I adore Communism, hell if I didn't wanna be so goddamn famous I'd brand the fuckin' symbol into my wrist."

"Are you kidding?" Derrick laughed.

"Hell, you guys, if you just read the fuckin' Communist Manifesto you'd see that Marx's ten planks are just changed words for America's view of international democracy, starting with taxes and social security and ending with public schools."

"Then we're Communists, we're all Communists," Viv retorted with a look of hunger and fatigue buried deep within the circles underneath her eyes.

"Well, I don't know about you two, but as long as we all have so much in common, I know you won't mind that I took the liberty of inviting Katia and Alex back here for *South by Southwest* 2000," Derrick laughed out loud.

"Ha ha, very funny, well in the wise words of an American Communist, 'None are more hopelessly enslaved, as those who falsely believe they are free...'"

"We'll right about now, I'm feeling incredibly enslaved," Derrick exclaimed.

"How do you figure upon that?" I laughed.

"Well, if I have to be a slave to feel this free of Katia and Alex, make me a slave forever."

"We are free!" yelled Vivian.

"We are goddamn free!" I screamed.

Derrick yelled, "Let's go eat."

Viv chimed back, "Let's go to Denny's."

Mel McCabe

Pint Nite at *Antone's*

He thunders. I swear to God his voice thunders when he sings. But its more than that, its not just singing. Never have Vivian and I agreed so wholeheartedly on one man's talent. It's always tit for tat with us two. She'll start swearing by the deep story lines and genuine nature of Garth Brooks and I'll try and top it with vows to sell my soul for a child by Tom Waits. Dolly versus Joni. Strait versus Hooker. Brooks and Dunn versus Fleetwood Mac and always back again to Garth and Tom. But we never warred over *him*, pitted him against another, liked him any less than the other.

He might even sound a little like Tom. I'm sorry Viv, but he does. That's the biggest compliment you can receive in my book. In some ways he's better than Tom. Now I must ask your forgiveness Mr. Waits, but *he* doesn't make me wanna cry all the time. Although his dancers do, make me wanna cry, cry from laughter that is. They love him more than we do. They would have to, as humans do not put themselves out there in such ludicrous and talked about poses for anything other than the intoxication of magic music, that coupled with a little plain old intoxicating liquor of course. But never in all my encounters with the various nightly bar clans of total inebriation, have I ever seen the contorted devotion for which this man's dancers will publicly humiliate themselves. That is love.

The man at the table next to me last Sunday wouldn't stop yelling over to his girlfriend across the table in between songs, "I got it. He sounds like Cocker."

Then she'd kick back at him, "I just can't believe *that* voice comes out of that man!"

"No, I got it! I got it! He sounds like Stevie Ray."

"I just can't believe that sound comes out of *that* body!"

"No, hon. I got it! He sounds just like Jon Lee Hooker!"

"I just can't believe that voice comes out of *that* man!"

"No wait. I got it. I really got it! He sounds like B.B. King!"

No. He doesn't. He *really* doesn't. I'll be honest. I do detect a little revived Cocker, maybe some Stevie, possibly a little Boom Boom, but no B.B. And yes, it *is* shocking. I know. It's downright freaky, but do we have to cut through the bass and drown out the Mambo drums? He *doesn't* look like his voice. I can't ream her too hard core though. I remember the first time I heard him, then the first time I saw him, the contradiction, and wondering if we had a Milli Vanilli at the local level on our hands.

I think I was at work. Yeah, it was that dead-end temp job and my left ear caught the first riff off a little genuine National Steel. I typed an address change for a Sallie Mae loan prisoner. Houston to Austin, they keepa comin, I smiled, tapped on the right side of my headphones and that voice thundered in. I think it was the first time in four weeks I lifted my fingers from the keyboard on an unscheduled coffee break and it wasn't even for coffee, the last lawful nectar of the Goddess. It was the Goddess's muse, that voice that had me griping my quickly snatched pencil in wait for the DJ to announce where I might be able to hear this man play. *Antone's*. That's where he played. Sunday. Every Sunday. Pint Nite. It would all be ironic later. It would all be so entertaining later. Who would have guessed? Those dancers. But then, that Friday, at the keyboard, on my shaky 'break,' it was nothing less than the best music I'd heard since leaving home two years earlier.

Back at the apartment, I told Viv, "Mark it down on your calendar! Sunday. This man is unbelievable. I don't know what he looks like but I have it all up here, imagined in my mind. Seventy-five years old, African American guy, been around the block too many times to count, leathered face, leathered heart. This dude *is* the blues. You're gonna shit a pumpkin, he's so liquid life. That growl, it's like…it's like…thunder.

I didn't keep on, like the lady at the table next to us last Sunday. I didn't profess the obvious incessantly, but only because we all deal with shock in different ways - normally the opposite of how you might act on the average. I'm loud. I'll admit it. So that makes my shock reaction take the shape of silence. Viv leaned in and asked, "Is that him?" as this kid walked up onstage. I turned amongst the pushy crowd and whispered, "No. No. That's not him." But it was. It is.

The voice *isn't* in the right body. The man is white, as day-glow as a white babe's behind and blond to top it off, blue-eyed, five foot seven tops and no older than twenty-nine max. He's a kid, a cute little white kid, in suspenders and a leprechaun hat, sometimes varied in his less aging outfit of overalls and no shirt, reminiscent of how your mom dressed your kid brother when he was four. But he's got a mouth, a mouth that opens to expel growl, grit, hard life, whiskey and the blues. He plays harmonica. Did I tell you he plays the harmonica? Well that's in addition to the National Steel and the saw. That's right, that tool you have in your garage and rarely use. But that harmonica, when you hook the amp to the cord, to the brass, to his lips and he blows, it makes you dizzy, puts you in awe. You don't even have to think, you just say the word harmonica after you've heard him, even just once, and years later and you can hear him playing it, blowing the fuckin' metal off the thing. Can you detect how much I hate the man? And I'm not even one of the dancers, those people *defy* the definition of 'shameless.'

I hardly know where to begin. I guess the lady with the sunglasses may appear the most obvious choice. She would love to know that she is thought of first, with lasting memory as the cheekest of the *Antone's* shakers. Cheek is not the right adjective though. No, I'd go with Freak. Viv would stretch it to wacky freaky. Imagine those people you see doing Tai Chi in the park, but on speed, in lycra, having just washed their hair with Herbal Essence, orging out in slow-moe and with unfettered belief that they *are* professional performance artists. Well take eight of 'em, transferred into a single vessel and you have the wacky freaky sunglasses lady, dancing for her man. She is inspired to move this way because of the man on stage, but she dances for her partner, the man in the wheelchair.

The man in the wheelchair is not a bad dancer, but he too, like the children are to the man with the magic flute, is drunk on that thunder. He begins the contortions, flapping his arms like a helicopter, spinning his chair about the sunglasses lady, until she can no longer control her Tai Chi speed freak poses and pounces onto the lap of his chair, or rather his lap in his chair and begins the series of GO GO backstroke swim moves from the late sixties, only stopping to run her fingers through her Tina Turner do. By the second set, whereupon Vivian and I are lucky if we have not wet ourselves with laughter, 'Sunny' has leapt off 'Wheels' and is knelt beside Wheels as they begin their six-song pre-choreographed vogue montage. Each extended hand movement is done with the sturdiest poker face, as if these moves are being performed for the Queen of England herself.

We have the swingers. Our diest of the die-hard groupies, dedicating each and every dance to Brian Setzer and his orchestra. No matter how slow the blues song or how sad the song, this couple insists on jump jiving. They are brave, they are decent swingers, they have swallowed every last jumping bean on the planet Earth and can't stand still. They are *almost* overshadowed by the four sixty-year-old men in pastel, flipped up, cool men collar polo shirts. We have pink (not to be confused with coral), coral, lavender, and mint green. All men wear Wranglers three sizes too small for their waists, cinched in with enormous gold star belts. They dance the blues to the Lindy hop. The man in lavender does break up the laughter with a rare twist with his arms extended above his head in a 'raise the roof' motion, always leading us to the 'piss our pants' stage. All other occupants on the floor are women, mostly in their twenties and early thirties and all pacing themselves to 'out dance' the girl to their right and to last the entire five hours in twelve exact replications of the 'screw me' sex dance as eyes gaze up at our thunder, the only time when they can gaze up, because he is on stage. Although it is apparent many would get on their knees if he so desired.

We do manage to rip our eyeballs off Sunny and Wheels, the Swing Kids, the cool Wrangling Lindys and the Sexy Dozen. Hell, there is a danger of laughing *too* hard, but nobody can die if Viv and I haven't. We must not risk the inebriation wearing off long enough to melt their adoring masks and notice our jeering. We could be beaten to a pulp by this motley crew. We cannot avoid *the voice* that causes such irrational behavior either. It would be most irrational to try to fight the thunder, the growl, the life in that voice, in that little package is nothing short of miraculous. It's Pint Nite at *Antone's* and this guy delivers. He sweats and he sways. He croons and he loves, he loves his band. He has the time of his life, performing for *us*. The voice often becomes too much for the mic and so he leaps off the stage, among the shameless, towards the bar, behind the bar and begins pouring shots, lining 'em up, only stopping the voice for a hard throw back to the throat.

Do I ever wonder how such a motley crew came to be? All gathered on the dance floor, at the table next door, at our table in fact. Well it's Sunday. We are the unemployed, staying out all night, in bed by five, five a.m. that is. You become crazy when you don't work. You drink a lot when you have no job, or drinking becomes your job or the voice makes you this way. You take your pick. We're all nuts, even the voice, or the Goddess was when she put that voice in that man. Maybe she was just smart, what's that over-used cliché? "Big things come in small packages.' And my Goddess, by no means should I imply that this ripped and weathered voice of the people was placed in a vessel of repulsion. It is a sweet boy's body. The flesh of Johnny Appleseed in fact, adorable, tattooed, I think with the hopes of gaining a little believability, but it doesn't. That 'bring him home to your Mama for Thanksgiving' boy with a voice, that Joe Cocker, Jon Lee Hooker, Stevie Ray Vaughn, Tom Waits voice has something more, something so much more, something that has Viv and I agreeing, agreeing for God's sake. We're talking Garth versus Tom. We're talking oil and water here and he brought it together. And he makes you think. He's the Goddess's greatest lesson for never assuming anything, never placing a face to the human, never judging before the tongue flicks the throat and expels the word, astounding with the sound. Because that is exactly what it is, thunder.

When I hear the rain begin to trickle and then shower onto the roof when I'm laying in my bed, I smile at the beauty of the night, the thought of how easily I am lulled to sleep by the cadence of the drops until I hear the thunder. The thunder causes me to bolt out from under the sheets. The thunder scares me, yet it entices me. It draws me to the window and has me counting 1- 2- 3- 4- lightning. And I am now at the window, watching the rain, living the night, waiting for the thunder. And it rips the sky in two and I can hear the faint sound growing louder of that brass being blown slowly, sadly in and out in long, almost everlasting breaths, until it is interrupted by the strum of the National Steel. I see pink, coral, lavender, mint green, swingers, Lindy hoppers, Wranglers, Wheels, sunglasses, a leprechaun hat, overalls, suspenders, blond hair and blue eyes, the dance of the shameless and two young women laughing the night away. It's Sunday's Pint Nite at *Antone's* and I can see it all in my mind, looking out my window at the lightning and listening to the sound of the thunder.

The Bug Killer

I can hardly believe I thought I could complete a gathering of stories on my experiences in Austin without dedicating a chapter to Vivian. At first, I justified my neglect by thinking to myself that Vivian has no desire to be famous, a concept so incredibly foreign to me that I have to remind myself of its potential existence. So why does one attempt to immortalize another through the magic of pen to paper, type to print, realistically in the nineties, through the computer, if she so does not wish it? Frankly, there is no Austin without Vivian. Viv and I are cousins, or so we say, because it is such an unfathomable concept to so many people whom we meet, that we have remained friends from the age of seven for the sheer sake of friendship, all arguments and the plethora of uncommalities cast to the winds of change. Sometimes

I can hardly believe it myself. I have known Vivian and her whole family for nearly twenty years, but then there it is staring me in the face, usually at Christmas time when Toni and I find ourselves more comfortable then we've ever imagined ourselves to be, unwrapping our gifts in the living room of *her* Aunt Nancy's, or just Aunt Nancy, laughing at a joke that can only be found funny to those who know, those who *are* family.

So when she called me from Los Angeles and told me she was thinking of moving down South, I could think of little reason for not joining her. It was really never so simple, but on paper, years later, it somehow seems that way and the way it seems, strangely becomes the truth. When I say that Vivian and I have so many differences, I cannot begin to expand upon the point. To those who know us better, they would be hard-pressed to find a political viewpoint, a moral aspect to our lives or a character trait for which we are searching for in men, varying from the other, but the little things, the simple things lie on very different grounds and yet they do not seem so important. All our different tastes in music and clothes, hair, and conflicting future visions of the two car garage versus the penthouse on Park Avenue, mean nothing in comparison to the things I have learned to rarely take for granted in my cousin. The woman is a bug killer. I am sure I have mentioned it before, but I cannot treasure this bug bravery enough.

I was pulling down a pair of flannel pajama pants from the top shelf in my closet. Toni had come out to visit and was already in bed engrossed in a *Sovereign Seven* comic book when I felt the carpet move beneath my feet. Jumping back to find a cockroach blindly wiggling its way back under the carpet, I slapped my hand over my mouth to prevent the already erupting scream and instead began to shake. Toni leapt from the bed to stare with parallel fear.

"Whadda we do?" I asked as I did not dare remove my gaze from the bug for fear of it disappearing and then reappearing in between my sheets at some secret time in the night.

"I don't know. You think we should wake up Vivian?" Toni whispered.

It was after two in the morning and Viv had been asleep for at least an hour, which explained her uncommon exhaustion as she rarely hit the pillow before me. "I just don't wanna wake her. She hasta work at five-thirty," I whined as I took two steps back and bent down on my haunches to see whether or not it had wings.

"Then you're gonna have to kill it," Toni exclaimed.

"Me? Just how the hell am I supposed to kill the thing? I can't kill it. Look at it. It's huge!" I said in an exasperated tone of voice.

"Just take one of your shoes and smash it," Toni said as she got down on the carpet and watched the roach crawl slowly about the floor with wonder that had now accompanied the fright.

"We're wakin' Viv up," I announced as I took a closer look, turned and went for the other room. I opened the door to her bedroom quite loudly, thinking that if she happened to wake up with the sight of the light or the loud unoiled creek of the door, she could hardly have been sleeping soundly. It would be far less my fault for summonsing her from the epochs of dreamland. She didn't wake to the door or the light though. Instead she lay face up toward the ceiling snoring louder than a chainsaw. I did not have the heart to wake her up completely so I just faintly whispered, "Vivian. Vivian? Are you awake?" She did not stir. I turned and said rather loudly as I walked out of the room, "I sure would be awake if I were snoring that loudly!"

"What happened?" Toni asked when I came back into the bedroom Vivianless with the slump of defeat upon my shoulders.

"She won't wake up," I frowned.

"Well, don't worry, I put a glass on him until we think of something else." Toni smiled up at me from the floor where she was studying the bug now squirming about his new cylinder house of glass.

"Amazing! I applaud your valor! We can totally wait 'til morning now!" I exclaimed.

"No we can't," corrected Toni. "Cockroaches can flatten their bodies flatter than a strand of thread. That's how they get under the carpet and under doors and inside the cracks in walls. This glass won't hold him if we don't keep an eye on him."

I pondered the validity of her statement and realized that even if there was not a shred of truth to the proclamation I would not get one ounce of sleep thinking the damn bug had escaped the glass and was crawling up the bed to sink its teeth into our throats. I turned away from my sister and walked up to Viv's bedroom door again, this time throwing it open and yelling, "Viv you have to get up! Get up!"

Viv pounced out of bed in a fog, wondering who had the gun to my head, "What? What's going on? Has there been an accident?"

"Yes," I shouted, thinking I had to make this sound serious by Vivian standards or risk getting punched in the stomach for rousing her, "There are bugs all over our apartment!"

"What? Are you kidding? Oh my God! Where are they?"

"Well, I heard the others scratching through the walls, but I saw the Queen come outta my closet. You've gotta come quick, it's crawling all over my floor."

I scrounged up whatever energy I had left at three in the morning, that had not already been drained at the sight of the roach and did a pretty good rendition of someone running back into my bedroom as Viv followed at my heels. "Where is it?" she asked, spotting Toni hovering over the glass, pushing it in fact to keep the bug from thinning out to the width of that thread she was convinced could happen at any moment.

"Right there." I pointed over Toni's head.

"Gimme your shoe," she said. I handed her a tennie from the corner. She pulled up the glass and slammed the tennis shoe down three times before asking, "Where are the others?"

Toni and I looked up at her with unabashed reverie, followed by thoughts of starting a new religion to Vivian, the Goddess Bug Killer of the Western World. "The others?" I asked.

"I thought so," Viv smirked and turned to go back to bed.

"I'm sorry Viv!" I said as she passed the door.

"Viv?" Toni shouted out.

"What is it Toni?" Viv peeped her head past the corner.

"If you had a penis, I'd marry you!" Toni screamed.

Vivian thought nothing of being wakened and Toni and I drifted off into the land of dreams from where we had taken Viv moments before. This would not be the last time Viv would put up with my squeamish ways and not the first time she had demonstrated the quality of the most wanted roommate and honorary cousin.

I had been talking about wanting to go and see *Boogie Nights* since the first preview aired on screen three months before its release. We pulled up in front of the theater to find a rare parking space. I set my foot out of the car and onto the cement to feel something jump up on my calve. It was a cricket. I hate those things. I screamed and jumped back into the car.

"Viv!" I yelled as she had already closed the driver's side and was giving a quizzical glance through the window as to why I had gotten back inside. "I can't get out of the car. There's a cricket on my side," I yelled through the glass.

"I hate to tell you this George, but there are crickets all over the front of the theater. Come on, we'll just run," Viv said in a faithful attempt to coax me out of the car. When that didn't work, she reminded me of the hole in her floorboard and the likelihood of a cricket finding its way inside the car as I sat there in false security. I leaped out and made a mad dash for the ticket line. Viv sauntered up behind me, without rolling her eyes in the manner I knew I would have, had I had a friend with such ludicrous fears and concerns. I spent the rest of my time in line hopping about like a woman with a severe bladder infection or a blinding love for the musical *Riverdance*, as the bugs attempted to cling to the heat of my body. All other patrons in line just stood there like dead zombies, already numb to the activity that lay below their feet. I vowed that I would never become desensitized to the Texas bugs of summer and we entered the theater after, what seemed like no less than a year of waiting and jumping. Just before the previews, we sat down and I pulled our stash out from my enormous purse: licorice ropes, a senior box of Junior Mints, a carton of Whoppers, and a hulking bar of milk chocolate with almonds. Slumping down into my seat, I looked up to tell Viv, "You know, when I went to the bathroom at home, there was a candle burning at the back of the toilet."

"Yeah I know, I lit it after I had gone, but you blew it out after you went to the bathroom, right?" Viv asked me.

"Wrong," I said with a laugh.

"You really left it burning?" Viv questioned.

"Yeah. You think there'll be a problem with it for a few hours?"

"Well, I'll be right back," Viv whispered as the previews started and I watched her slink out of the theater. Where was she going? Maybe she was calling our apartment manager to go and blow it out. It *was* kind of low on the wax. I wished I had remembered to blow it out. We'd both have to just go home and see the movie later when she came back from the bathroom. After the fifteen previews and a good ten minutes into the life of Dirk Diggler, (the star of *Boogie Nights*) I began to worry that Viv might have fallen into the toilet and drifted out into the ocean. There was no way she drove all the way back home. I doubted they'd let her back in again without paying a second time. Before I could think of a dozen other things that might have happened, there she was sitting right back down in her seat again.

"Did I miss anything?" she asked, a little out of breath.

"Where the hell did you go?" I asked as I tried to sum up the complicated story plot of Marky Mark, the porn king and Burt Reynolds, the pimp.

"I blew out the candle," Viv said casually as she reached for a red rope and directed her eyes back up toward the screen. I, on the other hand, could not concentrate on the movie for at least another four minutes. She blew out the candle? She had gone home to rectify *my* wrong! She hauled her cookies all the way back to our apartment to go blow out the candle that *I* had left burning. She hadn't made me leave. She didn't care that she had to go down and talk to the theater guy to make sure he'd let her back in after running out. She had missed the first ten minutes of the movie and let me sit there watching it, let me stuff my face with Whoppers as I sank into the plush velvet theater seat. It was with that random act that I knew Viv was like no other, my cousin, my friend that bug-killing candle-blower, the self-sacrificing girl who sometimes doesn't even know what it is that she does. She does good.

"Good?" Viv asks.

"Yeah, I said it was good, not great, but good. I mean I like donuts a whole hell of a lot better, but the wait was worth it. Whadda you think?" I asked as Viv sunk her teeth into another bite of the funnel cake.

"I love it. I think it's great." Viv relayed.

"Yeah, well I just hate all this powdered white shit that gets all over the place and then your fingers are left all sticky when all you wanna do is shove 'em back in your pockets," I said as I felt the white powder begin to crust onto my left cheek. "I'm just so glad we got to come back up for this. I swear to God, I love this thing. It just isn't Christmas in Austin without the *Trail of Lights*."

"Yeah, I know what you mean. There really isn't anything like this back home," Viv said as she blew on the palms of her hands and rubbed the rest of the sugar away from her fingertips.

I watched Santa through the window of the make-shift workshop with a little boy on his lap and the extensive line of kids coming out the door just waiting to tell him they needed the new walk, talk and take a piss doll by Mattel. "There is Candy Cane Lane down in Palo Alto and that little street, Lilac Lane I think it is, up in South City, but not as many people have been going all out as they have in the past," I recalled as I could never forget the man who used to dress up as a reindeer back in the eighties and pass out candy canes to all the people who'd come up to show their kids the lights.

"Yeah, it isn't *The Trail of Lights* though," Viv said as we stood up from the bench and walked through the last part of the circle. *The Trail of Lights* was a part of Austin that everyone from the retirement center had told us was a necessity of the holiday and they'd been right. We thought it'd be a series of lights thrown over a few trees, but oh no, this was serious business. The first year we had gone, the line of cars must have extended out a half a mile from the park and another quarter mile down along the feeder. We quickly assessed the situation as being far more than a rinky-dink set up. Once we found parking in the field, we followed the all-knowing crowd toward the streams of lights that must have extended at least a hundred feet up into the air, coming together to form a Christmas tree. Beyond the tree, an iron sign lit up to read *The Trail of Lights* in azure blue and lime green. We passed on underneath the sign and saw that a different company had each sponsored a plot of land and had done its best to outdo the next. Angels and animals, gingerbread houses, world globes and sleighs with Santa all in full Technicolor shining bright in the pitch-dark night. Vivian and I had not estimated the cold of the night. Hell, we didn't think Texans did all that much outside the comforts of their trucks and had been disillusioned into thinking the lights might be gazed at through the panes of our car windows. The cold added to the beauty though, warriorized us in a way it never failed to do and made just about every walker more than a little excited to go to Santa's workshop where the funnel cakes were good to some and great to others, the cider and coffee never failed to be described as anything short of magically hot and the lights were mystifying and fairy tale-like.

We come back each year for *The Trail of Lights*. One year isn't all that different from the other. It was probably the most ethereal the first time, because we had not known what to expect. Sometimes though, you find yourself returning to a place, not because you want it to blow you further out into the depths of the happy world, but because you want it to remain pretty much exactly as it did the initial moment you cast your eyes on it, predictable, beautiful and familiar, like home. On Christmas in Austin, even Viv and I find ourselves inadvertently creating what some humans crave and cannot find semblance without, tradition.

Following tradition, I push the last of my whispies into a construction worker orange sock hat and Viv searches for her gloves before the door is locked behind us and we set out upon the evening walk. The two of us have always been athletes of sorts, Viv of course being too modest to say so, but I'll boldly admit it. We can dance too, if the truth be told, *really* shake a leg or two or maybe it's four, but anyway. Exercise will forever link the cousins beyond blood and push another piece of uncommon ground closer toward the formation of the imaginary family crest. Our pool back at the apartment was too small to swim laps, a fact for which we did not discover until we were in the pool and recognizing its all around depth as being four feet. Walking became the new exercise of choice. I knew I was holding Vivian back when we started. Don't get me wrong, I'm a fast walker, but Viv is a runner. Nevertheless, I was the girl with the 'low fluid in the knees, the brace wearer, and neither one of us could muster up enough stupidity to separate in the night with the Groper Rapist still on the prowl. So walking it was, mace in each hand, me paralyzing my step to a crawl, Viv wishing she could bust out into a gallop, until the day she suggested the unthinkable, "George?"

"What?" I asked as I swung my arms vigorously and looked to see that the shadow across the street was a dog and not a groper.

"You wanna just try and run a block?" Viv asked.

I thought for a minute as we continued on and figured I could stand to test the pain factor for a single block. "Well, I could try. I just don't know because although you mighta thought my knees the main problem, it's actually the ex-smoker asthma lungs that gimme the most problem." I explained.

"Well, you know you can learn how to breathe so that you won't have as many problems." Viv suggested.

"I could learn how to breathe differently?" I asked, unable to hide the shock.

"Yeah, I'll bet you are just concentrating on breathing *in* too much because you're probably pretty paranoid about not being able to get enough air *in*, when in reality you need to concentrate on getting the air *out*. You gotta push like this and stick your stomach out. That's a big problem with a lot of runners, they suck their stomachs in to stick their egos out and then they screw up their breathing." Viv said.

"Really?" I said as I thought over her explanation and determined that I did indeed spend most of my running time trying my damnedest to get as much air into my lungs as possible. "Okay, well let's try it," I offered and our walk turned into a jog.

Viv was right. I would never have believed it possible, but six weeks later I could run two blocks. Six months later, I could run two miles. Six months after that it was four and now I cannot imagine two days going by without a good run. It was the breathing.

Viv never had to walk again. Sometimes I miss it myself, because I can honestly say that I just don't find myself walking *anywhere* anymore. But the feeling when I run, that rush at the break of two miles when your body kicks in and feels like it could go on forever has been a gift to me. The gift from my personal trainer who ignored the knees and because she knew me, thought, 'This chick is a really good inhaler and I'll make a bet she has hardly had a shred of good exhale experience.' She was right. But it's more than that. Viv's ability to be able to get me to run showed how much more she knew of other people's limitations then they might even understand themselves. Hell, every time I do something new, I jump back into my characteristic look of shock upon detecting a new talent, but Vivian is never shocked by my talent, or anyone else's for that matter. I don't think she was ever taught to believe humans have limitations. For her, it's just a matter of finding the time. Being a friend of Vivian's you begin to comprehend, that what you wish for out loud is what you get. When you say you want to do something, it is done. If you want to go to Memphis, you find yourself walking down Beale Street. If you want to go to a club, do not trifle with the warrior woman if you are tired because you will be inhaling smoke from the next table at *Antone's*, two hours from the expelled admission. You wanna move, she's found the apartment guide. You wanna go see a movie? You already saw it. You're thinking of buying a truck, you're in the dealer's office and she's finagling him down. The woman is not one to bullshit. I guess that would be something we do not have in common, but I'm learning. Quite possibly, this is why

I found myself hauling my ass down South. I wanna be where it's happening and these days it ain't just Hollywood, it's wherever Viv is. The chick is a boomafied dream maker…

"I finished the seventh chapter," I said just before Christmas last year when I asked Viv to read it fresh off the printer. "Now just remember, it's a novel. It's completely fictional. I think you're gonna hate this chapter. I'm just not sure. I dunno." I protested and pounced around our tiny kitchen.

"Just give it to me," she said calmly as she walked off into my makeshift bedroom (the kitchen nook) and reappeared having finished it a half an hour later.

"Well?" I asked with horrified grandeur.

"I love it," Viv oozed with zealous nods of affirmation. "Don't think I didn't see me in that one character, but I just loved it!"

"What did you think about the poem with the…"

"Intergalactic cowboy superhero?" she finished my thought.

"Yeah," I wondered.

"It was so perfect, totally reminiscent of youth on the mountain, the wild ways of the river. I loved it." And there it was. I had my very own personal story editor. I had a character for each of my books, unafraid that the words she might spout would undoubtedly find their way through the chronicles of youth, unable to find fault in the psychotic behavior of my friends on paper and able to find veneration for that which I created. When you find a friend so kindred, she can only be your long lost cousin. So right on the mark because she sees that intergalactic cowboy for who he is. She knows just what you are trying to accomplish, sees your efforts limitlessly and expects nothing more of you than *you*, even when *you* do not think there is much left to expect. There are no more bugs to kill. There are no more adventures you'll ever only dream of, because your cousin will always stomp those creepers, rush at them rather than helplessly watch them crawl, smash the hourglass to end the slow drip of the sand, and change the course of time forever. She is the eighth superhero from Toni's collection of the *Sovereign Seven*, the spider-killer, the roach-stomper, the candle blower, the believer, the dream maker. And she does not dream. She idealizes and yet strangely her reality is a place in which dreams come true.

There was this sixteen-year-old girl I used to know when I was five. She taught me swim lessons up in the mountains, a time, which I can hardly remember, when I hardly knew how to swim, before the fascination of water somersaults had even come into play of my little world. She was going to be a doctor. She spoke of it incessantly, proudly, always keeping the whole pool community posted as to her application status and interview process. After undergraduate school she got a lot of calls about Med school and was all set to go after having picked one campus back East when she met someone, her future husband, the man of her dreams, the man who replaced her old dream.

He was a doctor. He swept her off her feet, whatever the hell that signifies to the modern world, gripping the modern woman. He wanted to get married right away, have kids, buy the house in the burbs and so she did too. She gave it all up for the man. She forgot how she had spoke of Med school, the incessant chatter of plans of twirling stethoscopes and cutting into cadavers, looking over charts and having little kids chime, 'Doctor, doctor, can you help me?' Who needed to become a doctor when you could marry one? Who would ever remember how often she spoke of her dream? The trouble was that later it shown on her face that it wasn't enough. The trouble was that later we all remembered. Today, in fact, we still do.

Much of my faith in the practiced promises of young women was lost when I was five, when I watched as my swim teacher and the good Doctor held their reception out on the cabana of the summer lodge. Yet almost all of it was regained in my cousin, the girl who never *said* she was going to become a doctor, but silently, diligently, knuckles to the grindstone, and two jobs a day, was becoming one. I don't know when it was that I figured out just how lucky I was to be able to spend that time with Viv in Austin. I got her at that one period in her life when she was not in school, taking the break in between undergrad and graduate school, the free spirit for which she had given us all the illusion she always was through the eight hour school day, the five hour lab day and the four hour evening job afterward. I had never known Vivian to not be working or perpetually busy at any day of the year, any minute of the day, but our time in Austin was different. It was then that I discovered that Viv wasn't doing all of it to merely become a doctor, not simply for the sake of having that MD cling to the last letter in her last name, she actually *wanted* to help people. She wanted to do it right then, not when she could legitimately hang the stethoscope from her neck carelessly during a shop at the grocery store just to intimidate men as I begged her to let me do now.

"I think I'm gonna go over and check out that retirement place across the street," she said to me the second day after we had moved into the new apartment and our backs were still quivering from moving the couch a fifth time to the third side of the room.

"What? You mean you wanna work there?" I intelligently asked, as my mind proved as tired as my body.

"No," Viv said cynically, "I was thinking of checking myself in or scoping out the older Austin men."

"Ha, ha. No, I think it sounds like a good idea," I retorted.

She had the job the next day as medical supervisor and was on her way to helping people even if it wasn't for her resume for school.

"Did you know that Kathie Lee began doing shows for charity at the age of five or six," Viv asked me.

"Yeah," I responded, "Well I know she does a lot for charity. She has some sort of women's center in New York City and I think she works there too."

"Well, I knew about that, but I mean, I saw this special on her a few days ago and she was already obsessed with raising money for charities from the time she knew how to talk. She would put on shows for the neighborhood and if she raised fifty-seven dollars that was what would go to the local homeless center," Viv said with admiration.

"Wow, that's pretty cool," I commented.

"I just think that is so amazing. Of course, I love to hear about people who have a ton of money doing a lot for good causes, but to be doing it when you don't have a lot seems to mean even more." Viv said.

I realized that in a nutshell, that *was* what Viv admired most. For all the reasons she didn't give a shit about becoming famous, obtaining her star on Hollywood Boulevard, her prints in front of Mann's Chinese Theater or her autograph scribbled in the books of teary-eyed children, she could still not avoid being recognized for all that she gave to her friends, family and even strangers, all that she gave even when she wasn't rolling in the dough. Viv *should* be famous. You must recognize her for her random acts of goodness, and I do not only mean killing bugs for me and catering to my failing memory of burning candles. She talks to people, goes to dinner with the old folks at the center and takes them on trips to Wal-Mart, stops and volunteers her jumper cables to stranded people in parking lots, invites people with no friends to the movies and hockey games, bakes cookies for her co-workers when she hardly knows how to bake, pays off friends' credit cards, co-signs car loans, works double shifts for co-workers who want to go home and spend time with their wives and husbands, works Thanksgiving, donates money to the church, helps people with their weight adjustments at the gym and even speaks to those who wear spandex and seventies sweatbands.

Now before I nominate the girl to sainthood status, I will say that I did recently hear her call a nun a bitch, not to her face of course, but to my face. I point this out and put it on paper because I am on the opposite end of the do-gooders, a needy shit-disturber determined to be destined and deserted among the fires with my friend. I mean everyone seems to know where I'm going and it ain't among the turning wheel in the sky. Gimme a break, can you kill me for wanting to see my cus among the lapping fires for a five minute break away from the coal shoveling?

The wings that help Viv soar above my swim teacher and the stethoscope that will soon swing from her neck, away from the accordance of George's laws of male intimidation, but to save underprivileged children with heart arrhythmia's, raise me back into my world of ideals, a world that has me believing that some people really *are* good, not because they *have* to be, not because others are watching them, but because they simply *want* to give that fifty-seven bucks to the homeless shelter. Who are these people? They're Kathie Lee and my roommate. She's the lady I have coffee with on the tube each morning at nine and the one who I cook eggs for in the morning. She's the one with her own clothing line at Target and my very own honorary cousin. She's Frank Gifford's wife and that honorary saint. We all know where those two go when its all over.

She goes back to her house in the Hamptons. She goes back to her apartment in Austin. She goes and works the third shift at the retirement center. She gets off work to hit the thrift store at the pleas of her cousin. She watches her cousin pick up another end table for the already crowded living room and says nothing when she insists on rearranging the whole apartment just to display the new end table. The next week she finds herself in yet another thrift store and this time shows more enthusiasm at another piece of furniture they must attempt to shove into the Daihatsu and even nods at the weak argument that you can never have too many couches. She says nothing about the living room

207

appearing to have a mind of its own, spitting the chairs, couches, end tables and lamps from one side of the room to the other on any given day she may come home from work. The saint hardly protests when her cousin needs a hair model to test out her new manic panicking techniques. She accompanies the cousin with a grin and new head of hair to Hobby Lobbie, to Gardenrange, to Target on a weekly basis for nothing more than the hell of perusing the stores for the sport of it.

The sport is redefined and thoughts of Olympic contention are questioned on blue-light special night one Sunday at Gardenrange. "Viv, look at this comforter!" I holler over to the picture frame isle where Viv's new locks are glowing under the florescent lights. "Toni would shit a brick! It's all leopard print! I wish it was on blue-light special."

"Well, how do we know it isn't?" Viv asks in her scientific manner.

"They announce a different isle every half hour and then you have to go and find a ticket person with a red shirt to give you a half-off tag." I explain.

"I know, but how do you know where the person is gonna be in the store?" Viv asks.

"Well, that's the whole fun of the thang. You have no clue. So it's kinda like a free for all, run to attack the poor red shirt lady." I laugh out.

"*Pillow isle blue-light special. Thirty minutes starting now*," a nasally voice yells out over the intercom.

Viv grabs the comforter and takes off like a cheetah with the animal print held close to her chest. "Where are you going?" I yell out.

"We gotta find her!" she hollers out, rapidly turning her head at each isle, making faster time than the woman who freaked out about the doilies the previous Sunday and the man who needed the glue gun the Sunday before that.

Five minutes later, I find Vivian in the fake flower and leaf section arguing with a red shirt over the logistics of comforters indeed being part of the pillow isle. She loses the battle, but not without ingraining a permanent memory of the speed with which that girl took off for her ticket. I created a monster, a intergalactic cowboy of the bargain bonanza, once again throwing all thought of limitation to the sissy shopper.

Greedily eager to imagine my own star among the strip of Hollywood Boulevard, Viv finds me star-watching incessantly, whispering out my parallels of that man outside the Continental Club who looks just like Clint Eastwood, and that singer back at *Antone's* who could be Aretha. But that is all it is, the imagination of one lunatic, a lunatic who is never made to feel one, within the presence of her cousin, rarely laughed at, hardly ever taken any less seriously than those who have the privilege of remaining somehow sane on this insane planet. And so when I see myself, who I am, a woman without limitations around Vivian, remaining forever joined at the hip of this girl with whom I had my first holy communion (the one recognized by the church). I see Don Quixote with his faithful Sancho Panza. Now I know, this may not seem like the ideal parallel to Cervantes connoisseurs. Vivian is not a dimwit by any Panza standards and yet she allows me to make mistakes. She actually encourages me to gallop full-throttle with my lance held high, into the turning windmills of this century's treacherous terrain.

"Attack!" she screams from her own grand stallion, encouraging my delusions, truly believing as I do, that life is as *you* see it, and is what *you* make of it. Hell, life is even more than what you see before your eyes when your Viv's cousin. You can 'dream the impossible dream.' You can make it happen if to only utter the words out loud. Is conquering the roaches, any more of a crazy plight than conquering the imaginary knights of La Mancha? Is Tom Waits any less achievable than Dulcinea of El Toboso?

"What did you ever get out of being my friend?" I have always wanted to ask my cousin. She would probably then admit that I was her case study for the Neuroscience convention, a practice patient, yet another vestal of charity needing work. She may just smile and scream, "Attack, there is still hours left in the day, things to do, bugs to kill, candles to blow out, movies to see, furniture to buy, people to save!"

So, "Attack!" I shall scream back and rush the monster, charge the knights, crush the bugs in the wind. We dash about and race with the strong knees of those freshly born and the hearty breaths of Olympic champions. We hurry to see who can open up their gifts faster at Aunt Nancy's. We jump the lady with the red shirt, as they call out the blue-light special. We run faster away from the coast and into the heat of the heart of Texas. We rush to blow out the candles, past *The Trail of Lights*, the funnel cake stand, and Santa, marching quickly toward our futures, toward my dreams, and Viv's reality, where we are doctors and writers, charity workers and stars, pressing our hands into the fresh cement outside of Mann's Chinese Theater. And when we get there, when *I* get there, I shall but *only then* have time to look back and know that she will *not* be found where I am going. The lady is not destined for Fame. But I will sign her name next to my handprints anyway. Because any kind words that might save me from my spot among the hellions of Fame will be her's. Any good I may have accomplished before ascending the steps I will kneel before, at that place in time, will be due to a certain doctor, a special cousin, one true friend.

Mel McCabe

My heart on my sleeve,
My home in my pocket.

Vivian has these two pet birds. As of late, they each have their own way of making me ceaselessly rub the hell out of my ear, a trait that proves my neurosis to the core, but they do it. Tahoe possesses the capability to screech in the most horrific high-pitched manner that after a long five minutes has my ear nearly falling off the side of my face. Jordan, the true instigator of bad behavior, flies to the top of my head at every chance he gets, whereupon he digs his sharp little claws a good two layers beneath my hairline. It began as an only moderately annoying habit. I would bring something to eat in from the kitchen to the living room and felt as though I could understand his need to fly to the food. The logistics flew out the window faster than he made it to my head as the food began to matter very little and he just began to reside atop my mop at all times when I unlocked the cage. I will admit that all ill-effect would be cured if I could kick the ear rubbing habit, a tendency with far worse effects than nail biting, even the potentiality of becoming cancerous and of course the pure physical downfall in having one Dumbo ear by the ripe old age of thirty. Nevertheless, there are only so many habits I am capable of kicking in my twenties and so I must remain in a little pain.

I have gotten used to the birds. It is amazing how one can adjust when she is thrown into an environment. I probably spend more time with my feathered cohorts than any other living beings, having been told the goldfish does not count. There was a time not so long ago that the ear rubbing was the least of my problems and the cage could not even be left open for fear that I would kill myself after another attempt at hitting the deck when Jordan would lunge at me. It will be a long time before I make it to the status to which Viv has told me she is sure to find me in a year, biking down Santa Monica Boulevard with Jordan and Tahoe clinging onto a handle-bar each. Personally those people frighten me, more than a little. The birds may constitute my closest friends, but broadcasting it to the rest of the Los Angeles beach crew like some modern day grrl pirate is not my idea of masking the insanity. The birds are not a far cry from the bugs down here, an admission Viv would not be too happy about hearing. They are her babies and I would venture so far as to think that she hardly spots an inkling of bugginess in either one of them, but for me they are close cousins. They force me, just as the creepy-crawlers, to every day relinquish a piece of my fears, to change. Now that

I think of it, nearly everything down here has changed me. Not in the way I think most of my California friends and family thought the South might do, but in a good way, a strange way, in ways I never thought possible, to sound utterly cliché and positively Hallmark.

For all of these stories that may seem so unrelated to the average reader, they come together in a perfect puzzle for me, in the form of my life, in the cut and fit way my whole being has come together down here in this slacker town of slow comfort and southern enchantment. Because Austin is much more to me than a compilation of a dozen short stories, neatly bound in paper and sew together with thread. Austin is my home, a fact to which only became so clear to me once I had left, and yes, I did leave. I found myself, six months later, not geographically far from Austin, but in a city immensely distancing me from its seducing air, its coffee, its thunder and nightclubs that hugged me with more confidence than my own bed and its people that looked up at me with smiles that made me think I must have met that person somewhere before, even when I knew I hadn't.

It was indeed necessary for me to create distance and look back, as I find myself so often doing, with a sad smile and a mystical eye of wonderment at what had almost been lost, until I realized what had been gained. Memories. It is now when I look back at Austin that I see so much more than what it had been before my toes curled ten different ways into the grass of Zilker Park, more than just a tack on the map of places I wished I had been. It is now that I can laugh wholeheartedly, thinking of Vivian's expulsion at the road stop just outside of Phoenix.

"So what exactly are you worried about George?" Viv asked me as I scooted into the booth after Toni and glanced over at her and her brother, Matt, rolling his eyes again in utter disbelief that the melodrama rarely took a fiver from my face.

"I just don't know if maybe we should just drive another twenty miles or so into Phoenix and just set up camp there," I pleaded.

Matt looked up from his menu in bewilderment and asked, "You mean you wanna live in Phoenix?"

Viv remained the statue of poise and turned to Matt and said, "Well, I know we planned on heading out to Austin, but if she wants to go to Phoenix, let's stop by the next bookstore we spot and look up how many Med schools they have here in Arizona and what the rent is like."

"No, no, you are kidding Georgia! You guys are moving to Austin! Vivian, you are moving in with a crazy woman. I always knew it, but this is crazy, *really* crazy! Why aren't you just gonna go to Austin?" Matt yelled out as the waitress placed four waters down onto the table and turned back toward the counter to give us more time. She had already spotted the California plates as we pulled up and smiled that we had fulfilled her store-bought stereotypes of the fruity loons indigenous to the West Coast.

"She's just kidding," Toni chimed in, "She's scared and just being George."

And she was right. I was in fact more than scared, terrified, but of what exactly, I could not place. I only knew that despite the fact that there was nothing for me left at home, the thought of only being half as far away as we had set out to go, cast an illusion of further comfort. It did not matter that Phoenix was dry, hot, in the middle of the desert, a largely conservative town, predominantly white and in the only state that did not celebrate Martin Luther King Junior Day. I was being George, completely irrational and melodramatic. Thankfully, Vivian was being Vivian, unaffected by my unremitting banter and as always, allowing me to work out my fears for myself, resting more assured than my own sister that I would come to the rational conclusion in the end. Oddly, it was Viv's *very* indifference to the town in which we pitched our tent that made me think twice, thrice and fourice about whether or not I could just stop the car and begin the unpacking process in quite the same way she was making me believe that she could.

"Every town's the same to me," Viv said with a hundred and eighty degrees of lackluster in her voice.

I knew that there were not enough Med Schools in Arizona for Vivian to be telling the truth of the gods, but if there had been, I'm sure she would not have been any less happy in Phoenix than Austin. But the fact was that *all towns were not the same to me.*

I wasn't riding down South by the seat of my pants, eating up a half-baked idea, cruising upon the very coattails of my cousin for the shear fun of it. I was coming out to Austin, Texas because of the small taste of everything I had loved when I had first visited, the same bites that would turn into the meals for which I would acquire a hankering and could never be fully satisfied. It was the Cuban café and the way the capital building lit up at night from the base to the dome that glowed all the way down South Congress to the Continental. It was the friendly faces and the plethora of beautiful men with body piercings and tattoos, the massive blue snowcones and the Berkeliesk air of the whole place, but it was also something more. Sure it was about the adventure, the need to get away from home, plunge out into the unknown abyss, live life *before* I got married and had kids all with the comfort of being able to begin anew with one of my greatest friends. But even that was not the *reason* Austin called to me in a way unlike '*every other town.*'

I guess I should say that I am not sure if I *can* really explain it. This is probably one of the most shameful admissions for an aspiring writer and so I will *try* and make you understand. I believe that some people, i.e. Vivian, feel that a city is a city, fantastic, filled with possibility and completely up to the individual to make of it what she wants. This person believes that every town has its hot spots, artsy corners, quaint bookstores, comfy coffee shops, something within that town that can make it a spectacular place to live. This person also often believes that he or she could have a rewarding and fun-filled time in *any* city on the planet, often making the city better if only to have a friend or significant other to live within that metropolis. These people have never been to Detroit. I have.

My people believe that every city is a completely separate breathing organism within itself. We believe that there are certain towns for specific people. You like the blues - you belong in Memphis. You're into granola - you're a Portland girl. You're unaffected by depression and like coffee, hit rainy wired Seattle. You don't sleep and sing show tunes, go to New York. But it's more than that. For me, for others like me, there is a feeling, not merely a 'show tune, I like the beach, gimme the blues, coffee coffee,' kind of feeling, but an aura that smacks you in the face when you find yourself in a certain urban setting that has you holding everything inside back from having your furniture sent out on the spot because you want so badly to live there. And it is not *every* town that does this to you, but merely a few, a few that you've been to and a few others that you have a feeling might grasp you in the same way. And so you move there, to that city that you may have dreamt of as a child, seen pictures of as a teenager or visited once to have always wanted to return to again. I felt that way when I came out to Austin, not the first day, but the second and it was that very feeling that I sailed back toward after my burger at the truck stop, just outside of Phoenix. That is the feeling that saved Vivian from Phoenix (even if she still believes all cities are the same) and brought us one thousand miles further from the desert and the cacti, further from life under the Republican sun, further eastward to Austin, Texas.

So I suppose that's a small tip off the iceberg of necessary explanation, the glance through the window's view of the people who hear the land calling to them, not 'the land,' but rather a distinct plot on this immense asteroid. The rest is as follows: people who see little difference between New Orleans and Boise, see things differently than me or others like me. There are cities that open up their arms to visitors in ways that they do not for others. I believe San Francisco did that for my cousin Ted. I also think that our hometowns have a way of calling us back, no matter how fast we may have found ourselves fleeing at that ripe old age of eighteen, if only when we sense death breathing closer down our necks. I believe that New Orleans must howl out Mr. Waits' name in his dreams because he hasn't written too many songs that turn the corners of Tulsa or Kansas City or prove his inspirations in Denver or Atlanta. Yet he can croon on a good seedy strip of Bourbon Street and with the heart of Jersey and Jonesburg so much that I almost wish I were from those dreary places. My sister can entertain herself for hours recalling her trips from school to Verita's along the cobblestone streets of Firenze. The Christmas lights atop the cathedral of Fiesole nearly brought her back to Catholicism and the coffee enticed her to switch over from tea. Not a week goes by that I do not hear her speak of returning, forever or least of all long enough to find where she left her passion, the heart of my young sibling to which I see in my own dreams, floating beneath the Ponte Vecchio to the cadence of the Mandolin and the accordion as she sails her gondola along calm and narrow waters with gem-filled visions of the Uffizi. I see it so often in die-hard New Yorkers, the ones who can no longer avoid the six-month business trip in Los Angeles, enforced by the boss. Weeks later, we see them scowling along Sunset Boulevard, as though their skin is gonna peel away from their bones and the sunshine is scorching their very hearts. I've seen people taken off New York City with the shakes like a heroine addict detoxing without the methadone. There are cities to which some us find ourselves nothing short of addicts. There are towns like that too. They're on the shores of Lake

Huron, outside Chicago, deep in the cornfields of Indiana, in the burbs of Acron, Ohio and come tumbling back with the memories of the orange and brown leaves of Massachusetts. There are places among us that will not let go, not allow our memory to stray from our favorite park, coffeehouse, blues club, Sunday night Pint Nite, co-op, snow cone stand, bench at the shore, at the river, at the lake. They will not let us forget them without a slight pain in our chests and the dreams that prevent us from thinking of anything other than the day we may return. And I return, to the towns that spellbind me each night after dusk, in the land to which I must always return, that which lies beneath the lids of my own eyes.

I navigate the gondola beneath the bridges of Firenze where Giovani and his friend Giovani duo wave and blow kisses in the wind. I step from the boat and run to dry my bare feet from the water as it leaves prints along the stone streets of the French Quarter. Peeking my head within an ivy covered shutter window, I stare at the back of a curly-headed man crooning that the piano has been drinking as he inhales another shot of depression and exhales the life I am able to breathe in without guilt. A walk around the block places me just in front of my Parisian West End flat. Paint peeled red stairs expose black holes beneath the cherry and manage to lure me toward my bike that I use to peddle out of town. Through the French country-side, past poppies and bluebells, flowers that lead the wakened and recollecting Georgia to seriously doubt their existence in western Europe, but onward I bike, for in dreams all is bidden and positively nonsensical. Paris is close to the countryside. The

French countryside is not far from Prague and Czechoslovakia is a mere hop away from Indiana, where my cheeks brush against the wheat and the sound of the Union Pacific, blowing its whistle in the distance, sending me running like a raging bull through the perfectly rowed fields to hop a freight north, home to my grandparents, to the shores of Michigan, to the lake I always mistook for the ocean. I awake within my dream to find myself sitting up in bed, walls covered in red velvet, the sound of the fly trap zzzzzzaping its prey beneath the sill of my window. Crawling from my bed, down the wooden spiral banister, I open the door to find my uncle and my cousins beckoning me from the house into the lake, the only place to live in the moonlight of midnight in hot and humid July, until I dive down under the water and come back up to catch my breath in bed, resting on the floor of reality, the world outside of dreams.

I wake before I am able to return to Europe, before I can venture back to the sidewalk of artists, sketching portraits across from the castle, along the water in Prague. I wake before I can hop a plane or a bike, or carry myself on the two feet of my dream world to Holland where Amsterdam calls to me like a quivering needle to a vein, whether my eyes are closed or open. I wake before my dreams are able to satisfy all that is deemed my reality. I am forced to conclude that until I learn how to harness the beast that roams the world of my unconscious, until I can discover how to hold onto the reigns of the horses of my sleep more tightly, driving them into all the directions my unconscious wishes to go, *I* must go, physically and consciously journey to the lands to which I so desperately yearn to return. I must go to Firenze, to Paris, to Nice, London, Amsterdam, New York, New Orleans, the shores of Michigan, San Francisco and back to Austin. I must honor the feelings among the half who *do* believe a city is sometimes *not* just a city, it is your home.

These places may even constitute more than my home, because until I settle into one, they will continue to serve as something larger than the town that holds me accountable for a number on its population sign and a body in my house with a picket fence. They are my constants in the world of change I have created for myself. For as my honorary cousin has taught me, there are not enough hours in one day. There are far to many adventures left unconquered. You must dream the impossible dream. 'Attack!' and never look back.

And so I will, fearlessly ride off into the sunset, with Sancho Panza, encouraging my insanity and Toni the Kid, convincing me that we could go even faster if I would only learn how to fly. Our theme song sounds something like the sound of thunder, our mascot is a bug and our pit stop is a Cuban café. I will begin to listen to the call of the land by returning to that which remains closest to me right now. Austin. A town that has inspired me at this stage in my life, to chose it over London, a fact that bewilders Vivian, in that she knows I believe all things British are kissed by the very lips of the gods. But I return to the town where the memories have swelled inside my head so immensely that all that can be done to soothe the pressure is to cut a hole and let them spill out onto the paper. And I do.

I tell you that big things do come in small packages. Never know what to expect. There are grizzled voices erupting from the bodies of small white men. Home can be found in your favorite seat at the bar, *without* a drink in your hand, but instead with the familiar sound of a burning harmonica being blown in your ear. Some people never get sick of pancakes, I think I am one of them. Always grab a juice from the Juice Pusher. Don't ignore the bugs outside the Movie Theater. Recognize that being used to them doesn't make you any less brave to those who aren't. The United States is a Communist country and none are more hopelessly enslaved, as those who falsely believe they are free. Denny's is the same as IHOP, even though Alex doesn't think so. You're gonna meet people in your life whom you might not like, but you may have to spend time with them anyway, unless you are braver than me. At least once in your life, you will watch a friend walk away from you and know that you will probably not see her again. The friends we leave behind have a way of coming with us. A part of me lives in the Congo, hides in the bushes and remembers a time shock had value and surprises were fun. It might have been easy to have been a Communist had I not always wanted *so* much. Solace can be found in a cup of caffeine and self-discovery can be made at the chair in which you sit while you drink it. Sometimes the worst days of our lives, later become the funniest. If your friend is sad, fall down. The slow drone in a man's baritone voice is sometimes enough to make me believe I could wake up to the same face for fifty years. Stereotypes must be abandoned. I'm gonna go network the planet. If I'm never ready to go home, I don't have to click my heels to know I'm already there. My home is in my pocket and my heart is on my sleeve. Europe can wait when there's Christmas lights and funnel cake right here. The Ponte Vecchio will sail me away next summer. I'll wait until Londoners discover toothpaste. For today there's carnival rides at the rodeo, an old Betty Davis movie playing at *The Paramount*, bugs to stomp, blue-light specials at Gardenrange, Jon Dee at the Continental, hot chai at the Cuban café, cranberry pancakes at Kerbey Lane, cheap fast sushi on Guadalupe, a spot on the lawn at the park and Vivian telling me its time to go, go jump in my pocket and find the corner I shall call home.

Mel McCabe

About the Author

Mel McCabe is a freelance writer born in San Francisco, California, in 1974. She has also written *The Doldrums: A story of youth in 'uneasia'* (2000). She graduated from a small Northern California college with a degree in English Literature and an emphasis on poetry and Women's Studies. She is currently devoting much time to songwriting and other musical pursuits.